THE GREAT UNWASHED

[THOMAS WRIGHT]

THE

GREAT UNWASHED

BY

THE JOURNEYMAN ENGINEER

[1868]

FRANK CASS & CO LTD
LONDON *1970*

ISBN 0 7146 2427 6

First Published 1868

(London: Tinsley Brothers, *18 Catherine Street,*
Strand, 1868)

Published in the United Kingdom by

FRANK CASS & CO LTD

67 Great Russell Street, London W C 1

PRINTED IN THE UNITED STATES OF AMERICA
by SENTRY PRESS, NEW YORK, N. Y. 10019

THE GREAT UNWASHED.

THE

GREAT UNWASHED.

BY

THE JOURNEYMAN ENGINEER,

AUTHOR OF " SOME HABITS AND CUSTOMS OF THE WORKING CLASSES," ETC.

LONDON:

TINSLEY BROTHERS, 18 CATHERINE STREET, STRAND.

1868.

TO

"MY SINFUL COMPANION,"

JAMES DAVIES,

𝔍 𝔡𝔢𝔡𝔦𝔠𝔞𝔱𝔢 𝔱𝔥𝔦𝔰 𝔙𝔬𝔩𝔲𝔪𝔢,

AS A SLIGHT BUT AFFECTIONATE MEMORIAL OF OUR LONG-

STANDING FRIENDSHIP ;

AND

MORE PARTICULARLY OF THAT HAPPY PERIOD WHICH THE

PHRASE I HERE COUPLE WITH HIS NAME WILL

EVER RECALL TO OUR REMEMBRANCE.

PREFACE.

———

A PROVERBIAL, epigrammatic, or, in a word, a "taking" title is admittedly an important consideration when publishing a book; and to secure this quality all sense of fitness is often sacrificed. But while in the present instance I voluntarily confess that I have selected my title under the impression that it is a somewhat striking one, I trust to be able to show that it is also specially appropriate.

I am not sufficiently well versed in the history of stock phrases to know who invented the one of "the great unwashed." But however it originated, or in whatever spirit it was first applied as a description of the working classes, certain it is that it is a most expressive one—one the aptness of which none recognise more readily than the working classes themselves; and, indeed, it is just possible that it may be a paraphrase of their own saying, that a working man is one who has black hands to earn white money. It exactly embodies the working-class idea of themselves, excluding, as it does, not only the " counterskipper" class, whom the great unwashed regard (unjustly perhaps) as their inferiors, but also professional men, merchants, M.P.s, and others who, though claiming to be, and in the literal sense really being, working men, are by the unwashed workers looked upon as " swells."

The title of the present work, I therefore take it, is a peculiarly fitting one for a book treating of life among the working classes; and it is not in defence but explanation of it that I speak, so that it may be understood that whenever in the following pages I speak of working men, or the working classes, it is in the " great-unwashed" sense that I do so.

I have written in the first person, but it is in a spirit the reverse of egotistical that I have done so, the idea of the grandly authoritative " we" being too much for me. If in any place I appear to speak arrogantly, I beg that readers will believe that I have not intended to do so, and that they will be kind enough to remember that I am at any rate practically acquainted with the classes of whom I write.

The substance of the papers " Out of Collar" and " Tramps and Tramping" originally appeared in *All the Year Round*, in the shape of an article bearing the title of the first-named paper, the matter being now reprinted by the kind permission of the Conductor of that periodical. " Our Court" is, by the permission of the proprietors, reprinted from *Chambers's Journal*. The other papers in the second division of the book, and the one on Trade Unionism in the first, are—also by permission—reprinted from the *Star* newspaper.

CONTENTS.

PART I.

THE GREAT UNWASHED IN THEIR PUBLIC RELATIONS.

PART II.

PHASES OF THE INNER LIFE OF THE GREAT UNWASHED.

THE GREAT UNWASHED.

PART I.

THE GREAT UNWASHED IN THEIR PUBLIC RELATIONS.

WORKING MEN.

FOR a long time "the working man" was, if not the sole, at any rate the most prominent, subject of public observation and discussion; and though "questions of the day" occasionally put him, comparatively speaking, in the shade, he always remains a stock "object of interest," and from time to time again comes with a rush into the very foremost place in public interest in connection with questions in which he either is or is said to be specially interested. From being thus situated, he has been spoken and written about and *at* to an incalculable extent; but to those who best know the working classes—the better educated and more intelligent members, namely, of those classes—most of this talk only proves that those who utter it either do not understand or wilfully misrepresent the subject. Those who profess to be the champions of the working man, and the exponents of his opinions, speak with so great an assumption of authority, and in such a Sir-Oracle strain, as to impress most people outside the working classes with the belief that all that they say *is* gospel. The contrary, however, is the case. The oratorical and pen-and-ink portraits of their hero, which professional and self-constituted "friends of the working man" give to the public, bear about the same relation to working men of real life as the virtuous peasant of the blood-and-thunder drama, who "dangs" his buttons, defeats the machinations of "the libertine lord," and finally marries the Watteau-costumed "rose of the village," and in conjunction with her receives the benedictory laying-on of hands, and "Bless ye, my children!" of the heavy father, does to ordinary agricultural labourers. The best of these portraits are idealised from observations necessarily superficial and generally made with a view to their suiting some preconceived theory, while others are "adapted" to the interests of parties, or boldly evolved from an inner consciousness or a rich imagination, by persons who wish to *father* their own interested designs upon the working man. Thus, agriculturists, when trying to obtain a repeal of the (to them) obnoxious malt-tax, sentimentalise over "the poor man's glass of beer;" those who seek to legalise marriage with a deceased wife's sister assert that it is chiefly in the interests of the working classes that they do so; and the gang of roughs who, headed by the notorious Finlen, stormed the Home Office and held a rowdy meeting in it, as a matter of course also professed to be acting upon behalf of the working classes.

Now, such proceedings as these inflict great injury upon the working classes as they actually exist, since they place them in a false position in the estimation of other sections of society. The working man, as bodied forth by his professional friends, is endowed with such a number and variety of talents and virtues as are certainly not to be found in any other man. He is, on their showing, the salt of the earth, the only one man who has an absolute right to be in, or is really necessary to carrying on the work of, the world. In short, according to the gospel preached by his " friends," the working man is a perfect being; but working men as found in the cottage or workshop are unfortunately not able to " act as sich," and are consequently set-down as impostors, or unworthy members of the general body, whenever persons who have been under the impression that the noisy spouters or frothy writers who profess to represent working-class opinion really do so, happen to come across examples of the genuine article.

Again, working men have become so habituated to and so careless of all kinds of fanatical schemes and demands being fathered upon them, that those who notice such matters at all take them upon the grin-and-bear-it principle; and this silence upon their part, this want of *active* protest or repudiation, is naturally construed into acquiescence in the designs of those who are using them as a lever, and they are accordingly regarded as grasping, dissatisfied, unjust, and unreasonable.

The various stock-ideas of the working classes to which senseless or self-interested demagogues have given rise are as injurious to the classes in question as they are misleading to others. Those who admire or court, and those who fear or contemn, the working classes, alike speak of " the working man," and in the mode of reasoning which the use of this phrase indicates lies the chief source of the prevailing ignorance and misconception concerning the working classes. The absolute generalisation implied in the phrase becomes in this case mere idealism, and is totally inadequate to convey a just and comprehensive idea of those to whom it is applied. In no other section of society are there so many and such widely-differing castes as among the working classes. There are working men and working men in such infinite variety, that any one man embodying the distinguishing characteristics of the various types that go to make up the aggregation would be simply a monster of inconsistency. There is no typical working man. The phrase "the working man," though neat enough as a figure of speech, is utterly erroneous and misleading when employed, as it generally is, as a synonym for the working classes. People who talk of the working man would, if questioned upon the point, be found to have in their mind's-eye either an ideal conception, or some particular type of working man who is in many respects himself alone, and not a generally representative individual.

A list of the various kinds of working men would be almost as long as the Homeric catalogue of ships; so that, in speaking of them, *some* generalisation is necessary; but "the working man" is altogether too restrictive and non-characteristic. To be properly estimated, working men must be separated into at least three leading sections, the representatives of which may be respectively styled the educated working man, the intelligent artisan of the popular phrase, and Mr. Lowe's working man. The differences existing between these sections are marked and in kind, while those between the subdivisions that come under each of them are only in degree. An acquaintance with these sections, therefore, will incidentally involve a general knowledge of the working classes; and I now propose to give, so far as my abilities will permit me, some account of the distinguishing characteristics of each of these types.

The first of them is emphatically the best, and though not the strongest, is yet a large and rapidly-increasing division; and as it to a great extent makes up in moral weight for its comparative want of numbers, its influence in modifying opinion upon those questions which more particularly affect the social position or political interests of the working classes is now beginning to have a perceptible effect. The educated working man is the stock intelligent artisan improved and tempered by education. He is, unfortunately for his class, an accidental being, owing his existence not to any marked individual superiority in point of intellect, or to any national or other system of education applied to the working classes, but to some happy accident of taste or circumstance which leads to his continuing the work of education beyond the schoolhouse. From this point commences the divergence between the artisan who is intelligent in the educational as well as natural meaning of the word, and the artisan who is intelligent in the latter sense only. Among the working classes the work of education can only be begun at school; but the general body of them do not recognise this important fact. Without reflecting upon the subject, they have from tradition and habit come to believe that education should be and *is* begun, continued, and ended in school. Entertaining this belief, and entering upon a new phase of life on leaving school, they allow the work of education to lapse; the result being

that when they become men in years they are still
children in the matter of education, and however intelligent, naturally lack that expansion of mind and
increase of knowledge which education gives. There
are learned working men—men who are "up" in
abstruse sciences and various dead and modern lan-
guages—but they are exceptional; and I wish it to
be understood that, in speaking of educated working
men, I use the phrase not in a scholarly but general
sense—the sense in which an educated man means
one who, in addition to possessing at least average
mental capacity, is a well-read, well-informed member
of society, who has kept and is keeping pace with the
progress of the age; a man who, having class interests, is yet capable of taking a broad and tolerant
view of questions affecting those interests, and of
clearly expressing and giving reasons for his own
sentiments upon such questions; a man who can
find his greatest gratification in intellectual pursuits
and pleasures, and in his daily life displays in some
greater or lesser degree that refinement which education gives. It is of men of this type that the
educated section of the working classes consists. In
the majority of instances, these men have in early
youth happened to acquire a taste for reading. (I

say *happened* advisedly, for it is no part of any existing system of working-class education to create or
lead up to that taste for reading which is the germ
of all real education among working men.) This
taste has gone with them into the workshop, and
expanded with increased opportunities for obtaining
access to books. It has in many instances led to the
men availing themselves of the means of self-education
now within the reach of all classes, to systematically
improve their education in a technical as well as
general sense; and even where this has not been the
case, a diversified reading in standard and current
literature has had the effect of making these men
highly intelligent members of society; has, so to
speak, lifted them out of that narrower circle in
which the ideas of other sections of their class re-
volve, and, in increasing their knowledge, has given
them broader and juster views of life. In the read-
ing-rooms now attached to many large workshops,
in mechanics' institutions, free libraries, and a mar-
vellously cheap literature, working men have abundant means of gaining general knowledge, and making themselves acquainted with the history of past,
as well as of passing, times and opinions; and the

educated section of the working classes have availed themselves of their opportunities in these respects. As the means by which this general education can be achieved have rapidly increased of late years, a large proportion of the educated section of the working classes are at present young men, and it is perhaps more owing to this circumstance than to the comparative smallness of their number, that their influence has hitherto been but little felt in things political.

Among his mates, the educated working man is usually a man of mark. He is looked upon as a kind of animated encyclopædia, all such debated questions as it is supposed a "scholard" can decide being referred to him. He is expected to draw up all such documents as workshop notices, petitions, and subscription-lists, and to take a leading part in the matters to which they refer. But while trusting to him, and allowing him to exercise a considerable amount of influence in some matters, his mates are "down on him" in regard to others. They are inclined to think—and sometimes not altogether without reason—that he is a bit of a prig, or, as they put it, that he tries to "come the grand" over them.

The general tone of workshop life is, it must be confessed, apt to grate harshly upon a mind which is undergoing a process of refinement by education, and some of the better-educated among the working classes frequently give expression to their feelings on this point with an amount of impatience and contempt which is scarcely justifiable, and is certainly neither politic nor brotherly.

Again, as a principle, it ought to be the aim of educated working men to improve their class; but while the fact of their being educated does incidentally lead to the improvement of the body of which they are a part, their individual object is, as a rule, to improve themselves *out* of the working classes. This desire is commendable in itself, and may arise from the loftiest motives; but still, if a man is constantly expressing his intention to "get out of the shop" if possible, it is not surprising that many of his shopmates should attribute it rather to snobbishness than to what they would call such a "flowery" sentiment as a noble ambition.

Although from prudential reasons, and with a view to being so far as they can independent, educated working men are generally members of trade-

unions and benefit-societies, they are seldom what
are called good members. They do not frequent the
club-house on those ordinary lodge-nights when the
little formal business to be transacted is often made
the pretext for a more than convivial meeting; and
on special-business nights, when they do attend, it
is often with a view to taking-up some position of
antagonism to the general body, to hold them to
some rule they are inclined to over-ride, to "want to
know, you know," concerning doubtful official proceedings, or to tax the costs of delegates. By the
delegate class and professional "working men's
friends" educated working men are simply hated.
Being inclined to look suspiciously upon friendship
as a trade, they do not listen unquestioningly to the
voice of the charmer. Their admiration for polysyl-
lables is limited, and they would rather that their
alleged friends should tell them something more definite, even if less forcible, than that they will move
heaven and earth in their behalf; indeed, upon the
whole, they would infinitely prefer an occasional deed
to all the "tall talk" to which their friends treat their
class. They do not believe in lending themselves to
demonstrations and movements which, though said

to further the interests of their class, are really intended to show, and do show, the power of the
agitators who organise them. And they not only
object to support associations of which these same
agitators are the irresponsible managers, or subscribe
to the testimonial subscription-lists which are so constantly circulating among the working classes as to
suggest the existence of a mutual-testimonial society
among "the friends of the people," but sometimes,
by exploding the clap-trap of demagogues, by showing that, divested of stock phrases and "high-falutin"
periods, their orations mean nothing, they prevent
others from falling under their sway, and so "the
working man's friend" by profession abhors them.

In politics, too, educated working men sometimes
hold opinions that are regarded by other sections of
the working classes as traitorous. But though occasionally looked upon with suspicion, and having their
peculiar faults and weakness, theirs, as I have said,
is undoubtedly the best division of the working
classes, and has a beneficial influence upon the
general body.

In dwelling upon some of the chief points of difference between the educated workman and the stock

intelligent artisan, I have inferentially indicated some of the distinguishing characteristics of the latter, so that it will not be necessary to describe him separately at any great length. The representative intelligent artisan is a man who has in him "the makings" of a first-rate member of society. He is really intelligent in the primary meaning of the term, and from constantly being face to face with the realities of life— some of them very unpleasant realities—he acquires shrewdness; and these qualities of intelligence and shrewdness, I take it, make up that "rough common sense" which is put forward as his strong point, and of which, according to his admirers and flatterers, he possesses a monopoly. Now this rough common sense is undoubtedly a fine thing, but unless it is supplemented by education, it will not, in a highly-civilised state of society, place a man on a level with the age in which he lives; and this, strange as it may appear, is precisely the case of the intelligent artisan. He has rough common sense, but lacking that knowledge and that expansion of mind which education such as I have spoken of alone can give to a man in his rank of life, he retains opinions which, in comparison with those held on the same subjects by better-educated men, are bigoted, narrow-minded, and unjust. He is still influenced by stale, and as they relate to the present times false, traditions, and is easily led by any taking shibboleth which chimes in with, or neatly embodies what either are, or political wire-pullers tell him are, his views. The intelligent artisan is preëminently the political working man, not because he has any special bent towards politics or really knows anything about them, but because he is the most easily influenced by professional agitators. He is an impulsive man, unused to reasoning or drawing fine distinctions, and knows nothing of political economy or the constitution of society beyond the facts involving the abstract injustice to himself, that he who works hard, and whose labour is the active agent in the production of the national wealth, has often to endure great hardships for lack of a trifling portion of the riches he helps to create, while others who in no visible way aid in the work of production can command a superabundance of every good thing produced by the labour of others. And knowing and bitterly feeling all this without being able to reason upon it, and yet wishing to amend such a state of things, he eagerly believes in the universal remedies which political quacks assure him will have the desired effect.

In the matter of political opinion it is a noticeable fact that while the intelligent artisan is perfectly honest in holding his own views, he is altogether incapable of believing that another man in his own rank of life can honestly entertain views at variance with his; those who differ from him he looks upon as toadies or traitors. Nor will he be argued with. Once during my apprenticeship, when I was not so well aware of the last-mentioned circumstance as I subsequently became, I imprudently entered into an argument upon a phase of the bloated-aristocrat question with a thorough-going intelligent artisan. A nobleman who had taken a leading part in the politics of the county in which his estates and our workshops were situated had died. He had been a good man, a just landlord, a kind and liberal benefactor to the poor, and had lived a blameless private and honourable public life. On his death being mentioned among a group of us in the workshop, I, remembering these things, observed that many would miss him. To this my shopmate indignantly took exception, arguing that all aristocrats were encumbrances upon the face of the earth, and consequently could not possibly be missed when taken from it. Waiving the main point, I said, " Well, his widow will miss him, anyway;" but to this more limited proposition my friend also demurred. "Not she," he answered; "she's got plenty of money, she had no need to care; if it had been a working man, then you might have talked about his wife missing him." Still I suggested it was possible that natural feeling might exist even in an aristocrat, and that a wealthy as well as a poor woman might mourn for the loss of a good husband; whereupon my opponent, utterly outraged by the propounding of such an unorthodox idea, and my persistence in continuing the controversy, seized a heavy piece of wood and knocked me down with it. The lesson was an unpleasant one, but coupled with some after experience of a rather milder kind, it proved effectual, and taught me never to argue with a man whose political creed consists solely of class cries and ideas. Of the intelligent artisan's weakness on these points, of his impatience of contradiction, and the fixedness of his idea that all political beliefs save his own are wrong in themselves and dishonestly held, those who trade upon the credulity of the working classes are fully aware. Indeed they have been chiefly instrumental in developing these feelings, and they continue to pander to them. And thus it comes that the less-educated portions of the working classes, having unfortunately accepted their flatterers as their teachers, have not yet come to understand that one of the most needed of the many improvements necessary to any material and permanent elevation of their class is self-improvement.

It is for the behoof of the intelligent artisan that those terrifically "scathing" organs which profess to be the sole advocates of working-class rights still exist. It is for him that the Billingsgatish style of journalism is still maintained, and that the great " Alphabet" Crusher writes of the Reform Bill in this many-adjectived strain : "It is a bill ostensibly designed to enlarge the liberties of the befooled down-trodden and plundered millions, but really and cunningly intended to extend and perpetuate the tyrannies of the politically privileged, morally depraved, physically polluted, and intellectually sterile caste." Though not so ambitious as his educated brother, the intelligent artisan is less contented. The educated workman has in his leisure hours many means of raising himself above whatever is petty in his surroundings, while the intelligent artisan, wanting such means, is, if at all thoughtfully inclined, given to brood over the teachings of those who, with a view to supporting their own self-assumed character of the working man's only friend, tell him that the hand of every other man is designedly against him. In this way he often becomes a thoroughly discontented man, and regards other sections of society in a spirit of blind unreasoning antagonism.

But while he has many faults, the intelligent artisan has also many virtues. He is earnest and honest in his political beliefs, upright in his dealings with his fellow-men, and sober, industrious, prudent, and independent in his mode of life. Though bigoted in opinion, he is not selfish; for while he will make great personal sacrifices in support of his principles, it is on behalf of his class rather than of himself individually that he fights for those principles. His opinions upon social and political questions, though often wrong and unjust, are only so in being extreme, as they are generally founded on facts. His rough common sense protects him from entertaining opinions that are utterly untenable; but on the other hand,

his too great admiration of self-seeking spouters who
can " speak like a book," and too ready credence of
their bombastic vapourings, lead to his views becoming exaggerated and impracticable. And while his
virtues are innate, are part of the man, his faults are
in a great measure accidental and superficial ; and as
they arise chiefly from a want of education, there is
every prospect of their being eradicated.

Notwithstanding government apathy upon the
subject, and the want of any effectively-organised national system, education has of late years made very
considerable progress among the working classes, and
will in all probability advance still more rapidly in
future ; so that among the rising generation we may
reasonably calculate upon seeing the simply intelligent artisan merged into the educated workman.
The recent transfer to the working classes of a large
additional share of the electoral powers of the country
will also be greatly instrumental in improving the intelligent artisan. In the first blush of his new power
he will be almost certain to send to parliament some
of those friends of his who talk about doing such tre-
mendous things for him ; and the difference which he
will then see between the promises and performances

of that class of gentry will not only enlighten him as
to the hollowness of their pretentions, but likewise
tend generally to make him more practical in his political aims and aspirations.

With regard to the last and worst type of working man, it will, perhaps, be as well to say as little
as is consistent with a desire to avoid any conceal-
ment or shirking of the subject. If, when in the
course of his famous speech Mr. Lowe asked the
House of Commons whether, if they wished to find
drunkenness, ignorance, violence, and venality, they
would go to the top or bottom of the social tree to
seek them, he intended to assert by implication that
they were special and prominent characteristics of the
working classes generally—if his language amounted
to a statement to this effect, then he said what he
must have known to be substantially untrue. It
would be absurd to suppose that a man of his great
ability and knowledge of the world did not know
that any description of the working classes of this
country that attributed to them, as distinguishing
traits, such very undesirable qualities, would be ma-
nifestly false. It requires no special knowledge of
them to be aware of this. Their post-office savings-

banks, their building, coöperative, and benefit clubs,
and the general tenor of their life, even as it comes
before outsiders, sufficiently refute any such general
description of their body. If, however, Mr. Lowe
only meant to say—as he has distinctly stated he
did, and as, impartially considered in relation to the
circumstances to which it referred, his speech seems
to me to say for him—that a large amount of ignorance, drunkenness, venality, and violence would be
found among the poorer sections of the working
classes, he simply stated what every respectable
artisan knows — though, if he considers that he
owes it to his class to stand up for the idealised
type of working man, he may not be prepared to
admit—to be a truth. A painful truth, certainly;
and, for aught I know to the contrary, stated with
unnecessary bitterness, but still a truth. Although
it would be a gross libel upon the working classes
to describe them as generally drunken and ignorant, a great amount of drunkenness and ignorance
still exists among them; and though this, of course,
to some extent tells against the entire body, a large
proportion of it will be found centred in the poorer
sections of them. So that, taking the lower portions

of the working classes apart from the general body, it is unhappily an ower true tale to say that ignorance and drunkenness prevail among them to a marked extent. Not that these poorer sections are inherently more vicious than the more fortunately situated members of their own class, or than the wealthier grades of society, but because, as a rule, an almost brutish state of ignorance is an inevitable result of the abject poverty which surrounds them from their birth upwards; and this poverty, with the ignorance resulting from it, are the natural parents of drunkenness, violence, and venality. The prevalence among them of such obnoxious characteristics is perhaps less the fault of the poorer orders of the working classes than of adverse circumstances arising out of an unsatisfactory state of society; but from whatever cause or combination of causes such prevalence may arise, certain it is that it exists, and those who so blusteringly deny it are no true friends to the classes concerned. I am quite of opinion that he is an ill bird who fouls his own nest; but I also think that he is a very silly and wrong-headed bird who, finding his nest foul, hesitates to point out the blot with a view to its remova.. To admit that among the working classes there is a section to whom Mr. Lowe's unpleasant and much-abused description applies with truth may be painful, but it is necessary; for in this, as in other evils, the first step towards remedying it must be an uncompromising acknowledgment of its existence.

This worst division of the working classes is happily also the least, though, when its characteristics are considered, it must still be considered a grievously large one. The working man of this type has much in common with the rough, with whom, indeed, he is often confounded. He is frequently compelled to live in the low, disreputable neighbourhoods in which the roughs take up their quarters. His household is generally dirty and overcrowded; and it is probably this circumstance that in a great measure leads—in the first instance, at any rate—to his habitually loafing about public-houses and at street-corners when he is not at work. He is usually given to drunkenness, and often to wife-beating. He allows his children to "hang as they grow," not even taking the negative precaution of abstaining from blasphemous and indecent discourse in their presence; and it would be mere fatuity to attempt to deny that he would barter a vote for drink, or for a consideration take part in a physical exposition of *any* political opinions. It is principally in connection with these latter points that this type of working man is reprobated by other classes of society; but it is upon these matters that he is really least dangerous, and least difficult to deal with.

Both of the other sections of the working classes are earnest and honest in their political beliefs; and while they may differ on points of detail, they will at least act unanimously in seeing that the power now placed in their hands is not neutralised by the un- principled proceedings of the worst portion of the general body. It will be almost impossible to bribe, for political purposes, those of the working classes who are to any considerable extent bribable with- out the honest men becoming aware of it; and the latter will most unhesitatingly denounce and expose such proceedings, and by exposing, end them.

It is not from a technically political, but from a broad social point of view, that this lowest type of working man should be regarded. He is a canker upon our social system, for which that system, and its organisers and rulers, as well as, and perchance more than, himself, are responsible.

Of the working classes in the aggregate a great deal might be said. They are by no means *all* that the fancy of some of their indiscreet admirers has painted them; but if they have faults and weaknesses, they have also their good points. To a superficial observer they may appear a chronically discontented race; but look at their position, and ask if their lot is not one to justify much discontent. I do not wish to talk any nonsense about their having, as the active creators of wealth, the greatest right to it, or to preach the doctrine of equality. I suppose that

> " beneath the sun
> The many still must labour for the one ;
> 'Tis nature's doom."

But, admitting this, the position of the working classes still remains a most unsatisfactory one. It is not, I think, very theoretical to say that a man who works hard in some productive occupation all the best years of his life should, as the reward of his industry, be enabled to live decently through his working years, and to make a provision for the time when he is no longer able to work; but to the great majority of the working classes this is at present utterly impossible. Their whole life is often a constant struggle with the worst forms of poverty; and in the end they must either die in harness or become dependent upon forms of charity that are scarcely less bitter than death.

That all this might be altered, that social systems might, without injustice to any, be so rearranged that the will and capacity to work for the common good should command a comfortable living, I fully believe. The idea may seem a Utopian one, but it is not beyond the bounds of realisation; and though the day when it will be accomplished is probably yet afar off, come it will for a' that, if the working classes will only use the power now in their hands in a wise and tolerant spirit, and not forget, while seeking other amendments, that self-amendment is an essential element in any general improvement of their position.

WORKING MEN'S HOMES AND WIVES.

WHILE boasting of being preëminently practical, Englishmen also plume themselves upon certain specialities in the way of sentiment. At the first glance this may appear very inconsistent; but a little reflection will serve to show that their peculiar points of sentiment are at least "founded on fact;" so that to this extent they are practical even in these matters.

Though often exaggerated, the rule-Britannia-Britons-never-shall-be-slaves phase of national feeling is justified by history; and notwithstanding all that has been said by the reviewer, and done by some few of the girls of the period, the merry maids of England are even yet among the fairest in the garden of girls, and are in themselves a living justification of the pride with which we regard them.

Of the sentiments, however, that have come to be claimed as peculiarly English, the most thoroughly sentimental is that of *home*. I have seen it put forward as a matter for public congratulation, that no foreign language contained an exact equivalent for our word "home;" and however this may be, we are certainly inclined to credit ourselves with a monopoly of the reality. Considered in its broadly national aspect—in the yearning affection with which our colonists and others whose lot divides them from "the old country" continue to speak of it as home— sentiment and fact go hand-in-hand together on this point. But if we come to look at "the happy homes of England" in detail, it will, I fear, be found that they are *not* all that the national fancy has painted them. This peculiar home-feeling is supposed to be beyond the power of any mere wealth or station to give; is supposed, in fact, to be in itself capable of turning

> " Wilderness-row into Paradise-place,
> And Garlic-hill to Mount-pleasant."

Hence "the poet" sums up the philosophy of the home-sentiment by saying, " Be it ever so humble, there's no place like home." By this it is of course meant that, however humble a household may be in a general way, it is regarded as the brightest, most attractive, best-loved spot on earth by those whose home it is. But this idea is unhappily more pretty and poetical than true. Those whose homes are "ever so humble" are not generally inclined to indorse or act up to this idea; and indeed there are many of them who would be disposed to give the poet's line a reading totally opposed to the generally received one; who, as they looked round the miserable, filthy, overcrowded dens in which they are compelled to live, would be apt to say that, in bitter truth, there was no place like home—no place so wretched and unattractive.

Comfort is the one great essential to home; without it there can be no home in the best sense of the word: and yet in numberless humble dwellings it has no place—mess and muddle reigning in its stead. That the houses of the working classes are not what they ought to be and might be, has long been notorious; and we have at length had some practical legislation with a view to their improvement. The general opinion seems to be, that the class of houses in which labouring men are compelled to live is solely to blame in this matter; and to this point—the only one indeed on which it could be brought to bear—legislative action has been directed. But the style of a house, though an important, is still a secondary element in the constitution of a home. As

> " Stone walls do not a prison make,
>   Nor iron bars a cage ;"

so a house alone does not make a home. Among the working classes the *wife* makes the home. In no other rank of life are the home-influences so power-fully and directly felt. The working man's wife is also his housekeeper, cook, and several other single domestics rolled into one ; and on her being a man-aging or mismanaging woman depends whether a dwelling will be a home proper, or house which is not a home. Whatever sanatory or architectural improvements may be made in artisans' dwellings, it will still be found, while wives remain as they are, that of homes supported upon like incomes, one will be a veritable "little palace" in point of comfort, while another will be a domestic slough of despond. It may be said that all this implies that working men's wives are a bad, mismanaging lot ; but such is not my meaning. Relatively—considering their strictly-limited means, the want of special training, and the style of management seen among other classes—they may be said to be good housekeepers. The domestic faults, or perhaps it should be said misfortunes, of the average working man's wife are for the most part negative or non-conscious, or at the worst arise from her being to a certain extent imbued with the pernicious idea so prevalent in other grades of society, that the performance of housework is degrading. Her shortcomings are all summed up in saying that, though she is perhaps as good as could reasonably be expected from her surroundings and opportunities, she is not what for the sake of all concerned it is desirable she should be, and could easily be made. There are many wives who in these respects are all that could be wished; and nothing more strongly shows the necessity and possibility of improvement among the general body than a comparison of the household of one of these women with that of even an average housekeeper.

The necessity for, and advantages to be derived from, a technical education among working men are now being urged upon all hands; but there is a still greater need for such education among their wives. Women in the working classes have no organised educational means of qualifying themselves for the position of wives, plain sewing taught in charity or semi-charity schools being the nearest approach to anything of the kind. There are no schools of cookery in which young women might be taught something of the nature of our chief foods, and initiated into the principles and practices of economical cookery. No place where they could be shown that many savoury and nourishing dishes can be made out of what are generally looked upon as unpalatable, unmanageable odds and ends; and that consequently a family could occasionally have the luxury of butcher's meat even when they cannot purchase joints or steaks —beyond the cooking of which the culinary capabilities of many wives extend not. There is no existing means by which they can be systematically taught the care of children, or the application of broad, easily-understood sanatory laws to household health and comfort. And, looking at this state of affairs, the wonder is that the housekeeping of the working classes is as good as it is, and not that it is rarely as profitable as it might be. A woman in this rank of life has to pick up her knowledge of housekeeping *after* marriage, thus paying for experience at a time when she ought to be turning previously-

acquired knowledge to good account. This picking
up of housewifely acquirements is at all times a prob-
lematical affair, and at present the spirit of the age
seems to be specially against it.

A working man's choice of a wife usually lies between the domestic-servant class, and the "young
ladies" more or less directly attached to the dressmaking and millinery businesses, and unfortunately
both of these classes are not merely untrained in
domestic matters, but labour under the still worse
drawback of being, so to speak, mis-educated; so that
they have to unlearn as well as learn on becoming
wives. The shortcomings of female servants are so
well known, and are so frequently and prominently
before the public, that there is no need to dwell upon
them here. It may be that it is to a great extent a
case of like mistress like maid; but still when servants are either "above their business" or ignorant of
it to an extent that makes them "the greatest plague
of life" to their employers, it is evident that their
failings must tend to have a most injurious effect
upon the class in which they become wives and
mothers, and whose physical and social well-being lies
in a great measure in their hands. Domestic service,

though perhaps the best means largely available, is still a wofully deficient one for the training of working men's wives. A general servant in a small family that can really afford to keep a domestic, and in which there is a kind, active, capable mistress, will generally turn out well, and make a capital wife. But, as ill luck will have it, the general servant in most cases has not a mistress of this desirable stamp. She is usually the retainer of some poor housekeeper of the let-us-be-genteel-or-die class, who, herself regarding household work as a degradation, and not being able to employ an adequate number of servants, makes an utter drudge, a much-contemned "slavey," of the one she has got. Under such circumstances as these the general servant becomes a mere muddler, patient and willing, but slow and methodless; always working, yet never seeming to get through her work, and dirtying herself far more than she cleans anything else; and the working man who gets a woman of this kind for a wife is, to say the least of it, not specially blessed in his helpmate.

The subdivision of labour in those establishments in which a staff of servants are kept, though necessary, and an advantage to the employers, has not a

good effect when viewed in relation to working men's
wives, as it tends to make them women of one domestic idea.   If they are cooks, they are most likely
to be cooks and nothing more, and then not working
men's, but gentlemen's cooks—cooks who require expensive materials to work upon, and who are not up
to the only "made dishes" suitable to their married
rank in life; those, namely, in which the cheaper
and coarser kinds of food are made into dainty dishes
by strokes of culinary art to which gentlemen's cooks
are strangers.   A wife of this class looks upon cooking as the be-all and end-all of domestic management,
and speaks with pity or contempt of all other kinds
of wives as poor creatures who do not know how to
peel a potato properly.   The "poor creatures" of course
return the compliment, speaking of the cook-wife as
one of whom, when you have said she can cook a
bit, you have said all the good it is possible to say.
The housemaid will tell you that she (the cook) cannot make a bed or dust a room as it ought to be
done, while the nurse will "be sorry for her children,
if she has any."   Thus think and speak the wives,
each one regarding her special accomplishment as
the one thing needful to complete housekeeping,

but few of them being clever all round; and among them the working man but too often comes to the ground.

Bad as is the general run of domestic servants, the "young-lady" class is still worse. It is nothing if not genteel. Commonplace people may call its members shop- or work-girls, and slangy ones style them needle-drivers; but to themselves they are ever young ladies, and their business is "a genteel occupation." What counter-skippers are to the male creation, the young ladies of the needle-driving and cognate businesses are to the female. They are a class by themselves, are dressy, uneducated, frivolous, and affected, and are noticeable for trying to ape their betters even in the present age, when all classes do so more or less. They look with contempt upon domestic servants and service, and even when married regard household work as degrading, and are ashamed to be seen in its performance. On this latter point it might be observed, "And well they may!" Wives of this class say of themselves that they "are not fit to be seen" when they are at work; and they are right—they are not. They go about their housework in a mincing, muddling manner, and clad in some dirty, tawdry, half-worn finery, manner and dress combining to give them a thoroughly slovenly appearance, which contrasts very unfavourably with that of the really clever housewife, who goes actively about her work, and in her clean cotton working-gown looks to the full as comely and attractive as she does when "cleaned up" after her work is done, and is thus in a certain sense "beautiful for ever."

The young ladies are generally as romantic as they are genteel; and it is not until love's young dream of a noble suitor has been dispelled that they begin to realise the fact that they are probably destined to become wives in their own rank of life; and it is at the still later stage, when they have become worldly-wise enough to compare the income of the mechanic with that of the clerk or shopman, that they so far overcome their gentility as to think favourably —not to say designingly—of men who work at what in their romantic period they were wont to style "nasty black trades."

Unfortunately, however, for all parties concerned, the working men who would be the likeliest to make good wives out of young ladies who have come thus

far on the road to a better state of things, the men
who understand them best, and could let down their
young-ladyism gently, are the ones who most avoid
them when it comes to a question of matrimony. The
go-ahead young fellows, who when single knock
about, meeting the young ladies at the cheap dancing-
academies of which they are the belles, "doing the
grand" with them on Sundays, and generally fooling
them to the top of their bent, see so much of the frivolous side of their character that they are afraid to
risk marriage, being doubtful as to the good qualities
which in many instances really underlie all their
frivolity, and which they, knowing the girls, would be
more likely than any other men to draw out. It is
usually home-keeping youths, of homely wit, who fall
victims to the superficial charms of the young ladies,
and while "under the spell" plunge upon matrimony
with them.

Sometimes the young lady who has come to the
pass of marrying a man who is only steady and industrious, without being dashing or swellish, will be
sufficiently strong-minded to altogether put away
young-ladyish things; but generally they strive to
combine the young lady with the housewife, and

produce a trollop—a slovenly, muddling, unlovely
woman, who makes her home miserable and uncom-
fortable, and is often harshly treated in consequence.

A favourite idea with the young-lady class is to
continue to work at their business on their own
account after they are married, with a view to adding
to the family income; and in some cases, where they
are clever and energetic beyond the average, they do
so; but in most cases the idea is soon exploded. The
ordinary working dressmaker or milliner, if married,
can rarely earn sufficient by her needle to justify her
husband in keeping a servant for the household work;
and if she has to attend to that work herself it leaves
no time for any sewing save that required by the
family.

In speaking as I have done of a large class of
work-girls, I have had no wish to dwell unkindly
upon their faults, or in any way disparage their
general character. Speaking from a very considerable knowledge of the class, I have no hesitation in
saying that a very common idea that their morality
is of a lax order is substantially unjust. They are
dressy and vain, and often pretty and much tempted:

but as a rule they are virtuous in thought, word, and deed, while many of those who by vicious courses have brought discredit upon the body have really no claim to the sisterhood. And there are numbers of them who, with a self-sacrifice the nobleness of which, owing to the commonplace circumstances under which it is shown, is but little appreciated, work hard day and night to support parents or other relatives, and are emphatically good girls. All that I wish to do is to point out that at present their education, mode of life, and tone of thought tend in a special degree to unfit them for the position of working men's wives—the position to which, if they become wives at all, they are mostly destined.

Perhaps the best wife that a working man can get is one who is the daughter of a family which from its numbers or some other cause has necessitated her being kept at home to assist in its management. In this case the art of domestic management has grown with her growth, and she almost invariably makes a good wife.

Though of less consequence than the wife, the dwelling-house is still a most important feature in the constitution of a working man's home, and one in which improvement is greatly needed. The character of workmen's dwellings in the metropolis and other large and densely-populated places is as disgraceful to the age as it is physically and morally injurious to those who are compelled to live in them. They are built without any regard to sanatory laws, and, owing to their high rents, are often frightfully overcrowded. In order to remedy this in the London district, it has often been proposed that large employers should, with a view to supplying improved house-accommodation for the labouring classes, engage cottages for their workmen in suburban districts, and arrange with railway companies for the conveyance of the men. The only serious objection that could be offered to this plan would be that it would compel the men to carry out their food, a grave consideration for a working man's family, since a working man's wife who is a good manager will, by the economic cooking and spinning out of "odds and ends," furnish a dinner for the family at a cost little exceeding that which it takes to send out a dinner for the man. Besides, apart from the all-important consideration of its extra cost, a dinner cooked over-night and kept for several hours in a workshop is neither so palatable nor nourishing to a man as a warm and fresh-cooked dinner eaten at his home would be. But owing to the "plentiful lack" of labourers' dwellings in London, large numbers of working men are at present not only subjected to the expense and inconvenience of having to carry out their food, but have also to walk long distances to and from their work, and live in filthy, over-crowded, fever-breeding localities, where,

> " Packed in one reeking chamber,
> Man, maid, mother, and little ones lie."

And thousands of the more thoughtful and decent-minded of the labouring classes who, much against their will, are thus situated, would, were this suggestion carried out, gladly avail themselves of the substantial advantages to health and morality which it offers.

A very general idea, however, among the working classes of a comfortable dwelling-house is one in which a man can lie in bed until he hears the first bell ring in the morning (in most establishments there are two bells in the morning, one at ten minutes to six, and the other at six), and can take all his meals with his family; and to secure houses possessing these advantages many working men will put up with almost any inconvenience in other respects. Now there are many large employers of labour in the metropolitan districts who could, if they were so minded, provide improved dwellings having these highly-prized advantages for at least a portion of their workmen, and thus benefit not only their own workmen, but the working classes generally, by in some degree relieving the pressure upon over-crowded districts. Many of the largest workshops in the London district are situated in outlying localities where ground eligible for building sites is comparatively cheap and plentiful in the immediate neighbourhood of the shops, and considerable portions of this ground are often owned by the individuals or companies to whom the workshops belong; while in most cases they could easily purchase some of it. On these pieces of land employers might build a sufficient number of houses to accommodate comfortably thousands of working men and their families, and these houses could be let at rents which, though small compared with those charged in the crowded districts of London, would pay a fair percentage on the money they had cost. (This plan has been in action for many years past with the most beneficial results in connection with the large works of the London and North-Western Railway at Crewe and Wolverton, in which places the thousands of workmen employed in the workshops of this company would be as ill-housed as the labourers of London were it not for the relief afforded by "the company's houses.")

By attention to these matters, by a careful appropriation of all available ground in the immediate vicinity of workshops, and by relegating—so far as it could be done without oppressively interfering with personal freedom in the conduct of business—manufactories to outlying districts, much might be done to benefit the working classes. Houses for them would be more plentiful, and better suited to their special requirements. The house part of the question is one which legislation *can* reach, and with which it has already begun to deal—the one in which there is most hope for improvement.

While, however, untrained wives and bad and insufficient house-accommodation account for working men's homes generally not being as comfortable and attractive as they might be, improvident marriages are the chief cause of that utter abject body-and-soul-destroying poverty under which so many

of the working classes habitually labour, and of that
over-population which increases and perpetuates such
poverty.   In connection with this subject a great
deal of very injurious sentiment has been and is
talked. Marriage is the only comfort a poor man has;
God never sends mouths without meat to put into
them; what will keep one will keep two; and a
host of other vague sentimentalities are brought forward in palliation of marriages which common sense
and true humanity would alike condemn as nothing
less than wicked. A more practical apology is, that
as a working man's position will always probably remain the same, he may as well marry soon as late;
and that if he came to consider the matter on prudential grounds, he might remain unmarried for ever.
But this argument is only true under certain circumstances. While he is yet young enough to marry, an
average artisan may, by the exercise of ordinary pru-
dence and industry, furnish a home, have a few
pounds in the bank, be an established member of his
trade-union, and a benefit-society, and be in employment which, so far as he can judge, is likely to be regular. In this position he would be perfectly justified in taking upon himself the responsibilities of

married life; and if, from causes beyond his own control, poverty should subsequently overtake him, he is to be pitied, not blamed. Thousands and tens of thousands of artisans, however, marry when they are provided in none of these respects, and commencing their married lives in poverty, continue and end them in the same condition; and such men as these, if they are to be pitied, are also greatly to be blamed. Many marriages among the working classes are contracted under circumstances which are almost enough to make any thoughtful person wish that we had some restrictive legislation upon this point. For the murder of the child that has once breathed the breath of life, we punish sternly; but we stand helplessly, and often approvingly by, while marriages are consummated, the foreseen and inevitable result of which is to bring into the world children who lead a life which it is scarcely a figure of speech to describe as slow murder—and but too often murder of soul as well as body. In the upper and middle classes the man who married while unable to find a sufficiency of even the common necessaries of life for his wife and family would be regarded as something very like a selfish scoundrel; and it will be well for the working classes

when this tone of opinion exists among them instead
of the stultifying sentimentality and selfish action at
present prevailing with them on this subject. A
change in this direction is already taking place. At
one time it was the universal practice for a young
mechanic to marry immediately upon " coming out of
his time ;" and a generation ago a steady workman
could, if he chose, work a lifetime in the shop in
which he served his apprenticeship. But all this has
altered with the times. Any young fellow who in the
present day was to stay in the establishment in which
he was apprenticed more than six months after he
was out of his time would, in most trades, be regarded by his shopmates as a mean-spirited muff.
Knowing this, knowing that, in accordance with the
spirit of the age, they must travel on completing their
apprenticeship, and *not* knowing when or where they
may next get work, or how often, through fluctuations
of trade or the occurrence of opportunities for better-
ing themselves, they may have to change their places
of employment before settling down as staff hands in
a good establishment, the more thoughtful and intelligent of the rising generation of mechanics have
come to look upon an early marriage—save under ex-

ceptionally-favourable circumstances—as a clog upon a man's energies, at a time of life when untrammelled freedom of action enables him to turn his abilities to the most profitable account, and so make such provision as will justify him in subsequently undertaking the responsibilities of marriage, and enable him to meet such adverse contingencies as may arise when he is less able to " knock about."

The number of men, however, who act upon this principle is as yet very small compared with the general body of their class, and though their mode of procedure is highly beneficial to themselves, individually they have no perceptible effect in ameliorating the condition of the working classes at large. Improvident marriages are a grave subject for consideration to the working classes, and all who take an interest in their progress. They are important in their immediate consequences, and perhaps still more important as a part of the great population question—the social question which so far as the labouring classes are concerned puts all others in the shade.

The homes of the working classes generally are certainly not all that they might and ought to be;

but when the fluctuating circumstances of working men, their thoughtlessness upon the subject of marriage, and the utterly untrained state of their wives are considered, we should, while hoping for a better state of things, congratulate ourselves on their being no worse than they are.

WORKING MEN AND POLITICS.

For many years past the working classes have, politically speaking, been the most important of the three great sections into which society is usually divided. Hitherto, however, their importance has been of what may be called a cricket-ball order. They have been necessary to the great game of politics, as played in the Houses of Parliament and elsewhere; but only as an instrument of the game, not as players. They have been the object bandied about between the two great political parties, no matter which side was having its innings; and though (notwithstanding that they were always told that the game was for their benefit) they were disposed to regard themselves as being very much in the position of the frogs in the fable, they were practically unable to help themselves, having no effective voice in electing the players. But this state of things need no longer exist; the game has taken a turn which—to conclude the cricket-ball illustration—will enable them to send some of their own men to the wickets.

Recent legislation has given political power as well as importance to the working classes; and while others are asking, What will they do with it? it will be well for them to ask themselves what they can and ought to do with it. For though at the first glance seeming only good, this newly-acquired power is really a two-edged weapon, and will prove a good or evil thing to its possessors according as they use it wisely or otherwise.

Both by reason of their numbers, and as a class now holding the "balance of power," working men are undoubtedly the "new masters" of the political situation. Rightly considered, their position is one of grave responsibility; and it lies entirely with themselves to turn it to beneficial account. That they have the desire to use it for good, there can be no doubt; but they have yet in a great measure to acquire the knowledge necessary for doing so.

Politicians, unlike poets, are not born; they must be made, must be educated; and hitherto the poli-

tical education of the working classes has been very
scanty, and not of a kind calculated to ensure any
specially-wise exercise of the power now in their
hands. The only teachers to whom a large proportion of them would lend their ears have generally
been shallow, and often—either wilfully or through
ignorance—misleading. Many of them have been
toadies as well as teachers, and have by their proceedings so vitiated numbers of working men that
they either will not listen to, or at once, and without examination, set down as untrue, anything which
is not flatteringly favourable to their own views.

The labouring classes have frequently found
themselves utterly helpless against some misuse of
political power from which they have suffered in an
especial degree; and their teachers have taken advantage of this circumstance to represent such power
as a sort of elixir of social life, a universal remedy
for all its evils and anomalies. This view, to which
distance lent enchantment, has been largely accepted;
but it is scarcely necessary to say that it is a mistaken one, or that, now that working men have, so to
speak, obtained their philosopher's stone, they will
find that, though truly powerful, it is by no means

the all-potent thing they have imagined it to be. They will find, also, that the exercise of the power really belonging to it is not to be numbered among those things for which "no previous knowledge is necessary."

Grievous failures, mistakes, and disappointments will in all probability precede any practically beneficial application of it; and indeed such application is only *ultimately* possible on the supposition that the possession of the elective franchise will lead to their generally seeking a wider and more accurate acquaintance with the science of government than obtains among them at present. It is neither possible nor necessary that they should have the education of statesmen; but if they are to trust to political power as a means of ameliorating their condition, it is as necessary that they should, as it is possible that they may, possess such a degree of the requisite special knowledge as would fit them to make a judicious and independent use of such power.

Like many other students, they will have to commence their education by *un*learning. Hitherto they have been chiefly influenced—and not unfrequently cajoled—by some shibboleth of the hour; have habi-

tually viewed matters affecting the general body of
society from a strictly class point of view, and have
listened too readily to the voice of the charmers who
have pandered to their feeling of class antagonism.
In these respects they have not, perhaps, been worse
than other sections of society; but if, as they propose to themselves, they are to carry out the great
reforms that are yet needed to bring the practice of
our Constitution up to its (upon the whole) bene-
ficent theory, they must unlearn upon these points,
—must be better, wiser, and less selfish than pre-
ceding masters of the political situation. While
giving due attention to the great questions on which
party cries are founded, they must learn to steadily
look after the multitudinous details of mal-administration which go to make up the present general
inefficiency and extravagance of the actual work of
government. While seeking to benefit themselves
as a class, they should do so not in a class spirit,
but solely on grounds of general justice. They
must learn to consider the value of speeches apart
from rhetorical embellishments and stock phrases
about " brawny sons of toil," " the rights of labour,"
and so forth; and be prepared to listen to, and judge

with toleration, opinions opposed to their own. And above all, they must get rid of their exaggerated ideas of the capabilities of purely political power. It can be made to do an immense amount of good in the way of social regulation, but it cannot be made to override the laws of nature, or of necessity, for (despite the proverb) necessity has laws. It cannot, for instance, secure remunerative employment or a comfortable subsistence to all who are willing and able to work, when the lack of them arises—as they often do arise—from over-population, nor can it be made to conduce to the realisation of any scheme of the "liberty, equality, and fraternity" type. Equality does not exist naturally, and cannot be brought about by act of parliament.

Apart, however, from all visionary or transcendental schemes, the new masters have a great and noble work before them. When they have fairly settled to their work, the first matter that will engage their attention will probably be the wages question. The subject has been, and still remains, a most important one in this country, and much misery to the working classes, and ill feeling between them and other sections of society, have resulted from the constantly-recurring disputes arising out of it. Primarily, the question depends upon the laws of supply and demand; but as taxation as well as the state of the labour-market is an element in the cost of production, and the effects of foreign competition have now also to be taken into consideration, the subject presents a political and international as well as a social and trade aspect, and is doubly important in the former phase, inasmuch as its settlement would incidentally involve the discussion and adjustment of some of the vexed points of national expenditure. If it is true, as is currently believed among working men, that the total taxation of England is larger in proportion to the number of its inhabitants than that of any other country in Europe, and that the land bears a lesser share of it than is the case in most Continental nations, then there can be no doubt that the English workman is unfairly weighted. Wages must be judged by their purchasing power, not their nominal value; so that it may happen that the apparently high wages of English artisans, though really adding to the cost of goods manufactured in the British market, are in point of fact no better to those receiving them than those of the lower-paid but less heavily-taxed foreign workman are to him.

Some are disposed to over- and others to under-rate the effects of foreign competition upon the relations between English capital and labour; but there can be no doubt that the competition does exist; and the probabilities are that it will increase with the spread of free trade, and the extension and improvement of the manufacturing arts and the means of intercommunication. In any case British capitalists urge it as a reason for reducing the price of labour; and if a reduction on this score is necessary, then it behoves workmen to try to *untax* themselves to a corresponding extent.

That our taxation might be cut down to an appreciable extent without in any degree endangering the national dignity or safety, few will attempt to gainsay. Putting aside the question as to whether the scale of our establishment is not an unnecessarily expensive one, it is notorious that the funds of the nation have been, and still are, fearfully and wonderfully mismanaged. There are no reliable public accounts accessible to, and understandable by, the general body of the people. Those who make out such accounts as there are, are under the control of those who have the spending of the money, and the "lumping" manner in which the accounts are drawn up makes them of very little use even to the few who have time and opportunity to study them, so that "how our audit stands, who can tell?" But though wofully deficient as a whole, the public accounts give but too many proofs of the fact that the national funds are most disgracefully wasted. Perhaps no better (or worse) instance of this could be cited than a report showing the number of ships sold by the Admiralty from July 1859 to August 1867. Mr. Noble, the secretary of "The Financial Reform Union," has already commented upon the return in question, and as he has pointed out its significant features, I will quote from his letter, merely saying that I have verified—and in one instance corrected—his figures by comparing them with the report. After pointing to an instance in which the net amount received for a vessel officially valued at 510*l.* was 12*s.*, and observing that it would be thought impossible to surpass such a sample of mismanagement were it not for other matters in the report, he says: "An analysis of this return shows that twenty-five of the vessels

named in it were sold for a total of 24,621*l.* 0*s.* 4*d.*;
the Government, however, repurchased stores from
the same vessels, bearing the broad-arrow mark, for
the sum of 32,045*l.* 17*s.* 2*d.*, the result being a loss
of 7,424*l.* 16*s.* 10*d.* The actual loss to the nation,
however, is not shown unless the value of the ships
is added. Here we are puzzled. The return does
not give the value of eight of these ships, but of
seventeen only, which are estimated by the dockyard
officers as worth 24,458*l.*; this sum, added to the
7,424*l.* 16*s.* 10*d.*, shows a total loss of 31,882*l.* 16*s.* 8*d.*,
exclusive of the eight ships which were not valued."

It is a stock thing to say of watches that labour
under the suspicion of being more ornamental than
useful, that they sell those sort of things in Birmingham at 5*l.* a bushel, and a shovelful in to carry them
away. But here we have a case in which a number
of ships were literally given away, and a handsome
bonus paid to those who took them. The details of
several other transactions, exhibiting a like profligate
waste of money, are given in this notable report, and
conclusively show that the Admiralty officials are
either grossly incapable, or have been guilty of shameless wholesale jobbery. These things are bad enough

in themselves, but their worst feature consists in the fact that they are probably only specimens of "the way the money goes" in other departments.

It is to be feared too that waste, or even ordinary jobbery, are not the worst forms of the mal-administration of public money. The Count de Casabianca, referring to English financial affairs, in the course of a speech delivered in the French House of Legislature, and published in the *Moniteur*, said that "a special commission charged in 1822 by parliament to examine the accounts of the loans contracted between 1793 and 1816 and verify their employment, after several years of laborious investigation discovered a deficit of 53,168,600*l.* without being able to discover the authors of those enormous embezzlements. In the financial accounts between 1817 and 1824 there was a second deficiency of 8,772,400*l.*, without proceedings being taken against the culpable parties."

I do not know whether these statements are accurate; but whether they are or not it will probably be said that they refer to old-world matters. Unfortunately, however, they are matters of a kind that are not altogether impossible even in the present day. We are still without any properly organised audit-board; and while speaking in the House of Commons upon the naval estimates for 1868-69, Colonel Sykes observed, referring to the slave-trade, " The most extraordinary feature, however, was that, though the trade had died away, the system of bounties was still maintained. Thus for the year 1867-68 no less than 20,000*l.* was allocated by way of bounties for slaves caught. But no slaves whatever were caught: who, then, received the money?"

To this there was (in the *Times* report of the debate at least) no reply; and it is by no means a solitary question of this kind to which no answer has been given. To such matters as these the working classes, and tax-payers generally, must give earnest and constant attention if they wish to lighten their burdens. They must ascertain the opinions of those whom they wish to represent them, not only upon the Irish Church, or whatever may happen to be the " cry" question of the day, but also upon the always-important one of financial reform; and they must try to secure members who, when making such inquiries as that of Colonel Sykes, will *not* " allow the matter to drop" until they have obtained the information or explanation they require.

Retrenchment by means of improved management in the internal economy of the state will be a standing question permeating to a greater or lesser extent many others; but of distinct measures those relating to the equalisation of poor-rates, and the laws affecting adulteration, and short weights and measures, are the ones most immediately interesting to the general body of the working classes. That the poor-rates of a district should be made to increase in proportion to its poverty is simply monstrous. For this practice there can be no justification, whatever might be said in favour of a reversal of it. When the preachers of the grace-walking connection wanted to know *why* Colonel Quagg thrashed them, that redoubtable personage was wont to reply : " I licks ye because I kin, and because I like, and because ye'se critters that licks is good for." And it is upon the Quaggian principle that the existing system of levying poor-rates has been supported. Those who have maintained it and opposed equalisation have done so simply because they could, and because they liked, and because they had an interest in doing so.

Adulteration has become an almost universal " thing of custom;" and fraudulent weights and measures, if not quite so general, are yet by far too prevalent; and though all grades of society suffer from these evils, the working classes do so in an especial degree; and they are decidedly among the questions to which those classes should give particular attention. In the present days of extensive consumption sophistications may be necessary, or at any rate desirable in certain classes of goods, and a permissive adulteration, provided an avowal of the nature and *proportions* of the " mixture" were made compulsory, might be tolerated; but beyond this a line should be strictly drawn. The public should be furnished with some official agency by means of which they could readily, and with as little expense as possible, ascertain whether or not the goods they had purchased were of the quantity and quality for which they had been sold; and the punishment for fraudulent adulteration and the kindred crime of false weight should be made of a kind fairly calculated to act deterrently. For adulteration—a crime which, in addition to its other evils, has greatly injured our manufacturing interests in foreign markets—there is virtually no punishment, while the penalties inflicted upon those who are detected cheating by means of false weights are farcically small, especially when the profits arising from such a mode of swindling are considered. To fine a man five or ten shillings once in two or three years for practising a system of fraud by which he probably gains as many pounds per week is a flagrant mockery of justice, and seems very like adding insult to the injury already sustained by the defrauded. Confiscation of the adulterated goods, suspension or deprivation of licenses, a public branding of the swindling establishments, together with heavy fining, or imprisonment without the option of a fine, are the self-evident remedies for the twin crimes of adulteration and short weight. And if the working classes will only be energetic and true to their own interests, the day is not very far distant when these remedies will be applicable to the protection of the health and pockets of the public.

To give effect to their power the working classes must act combinedly; and to enable them to do so, their professional friends have advised them to use their trades' unions for political purposes. A moment's reflection must make the unwisdom of this advice apparent even to an outsider, while anyone having a practical acquaintance with trades' unions

will at once see that it is not merely unwise, but
dangerous also.   As the active representatives of
labour in the contests between it and capital, and
the sole managers of the financial and semi-judicial
functions incidental to the constitution of their societies, the unionists have already as much on hand
as they can well manage; and when the report of
the Trades' Union Commission has been issued, their
legitimate work will in all probability be—for some
considerable time at any rate—increased.   Politics
would simply be an element of discord in trades'
unions.   They could not be adequately discussed
save at the expense of neglecting those interests to
support which the unions were established; they
would give room for jobbery and wire-pulling which
would tend to demoralise the societies, and would
probably excite a political opposition which might be
injurious to the unions in trade matters.   And while
on the one hand politics might injure trade, on the
other trade could be made to injure politics.

Artisans naturally regard " the trade" as a para-
mount institution; and none are so thoroughly imbued with this feeling as are the unionists, who often
carry it to extremes ; so that a promise to go in for

guns and iron-clads might be used to catch the engineering vote, while a promise of fortifications or new public works might be made to influence the building-trade. Such considerations as these, however, are insignificant compared with the fact, that the trade unionists are not a tithe of the general body of the working classes. The unions are necessarily exclusive, and would probably keep out some of the men best qualified to take the lead in things political; and any distinct action upon their part would certainly tend to divide the working-class interest. In many trades there is a latent antagonism between the union and non- or anti-union workmen; and even though the political opinions of the latter agreed with those of the former, they would resent the idea of them acting officially for the general body, and getting the chief credit for whatever was done, while unskilled labourers would probably look upon it as a slight upon their class; and no one who really knows the working classes needs to be told that such jealousies as these might lead to a disastrous want of unity. In short, the cue of the trades' unions is to, scrupulously and upon principle, avoid all political action which has not a special and

direct bearing upon the purposes for which they were
originally formed.   An electoral or other purely
political association open equally to all working men,
whether unionists or non-unionists, mechanics or
labourers, is what is wanted to give effect to the
political power of the working classes.   In forming it
the constitution of the larger trade unions might on
many points be copied with advantage.   Like them
it should have a central office of management in
London, and branches in all parts of the kingdom.
Like them it should be entirely and exclusively managed by working men who are members of it; and
like them it should be entirely self-supporting.   Its
functions should be to collect all important parliamentary papers, and from time to time issue digests
of them showing their bearing on popular questions;
to select candidates for the seats in which there is a
reasonable chance of the working-class interest being
powerful enough to secure the return of a member;
and at election times to draw up a sort of political
catechism, which, while leaving candidates a fair
discretion, would elicit their general views and a
definite expression of opinion on any special question
of the day.   Such an association should be very

chary of making expensive demonstrations in the way of processions and banners, and it should carefully avoid being made an instrument of by self-seeking popularity-hunting spouters. In this last matter it may be observed the working classes have hitherto been very weak. It is enough to make any thoughtful working man blush to think of many of the men who are now before the world as champions of the working classes, leaders of the people, and so forth; to think of the opinion that others must form of working men if, judging by these leaders, they ask themselves what manner of men the led must be. The majority of these self-styled leaders are mere

> " haranguers of the throng,
> Who think to get preferment by the tongue ;"

or men who, even if their honesty of intention were admitted (and that would be a great admission), do not in point of intellect attain even to mediocrity, but emphatically belong to

> " the herd of such
> Who think too little, and who talk too much."

The leaders of a great people should themselves be great; should be men who have made their mark upon the age, and whose individual greatness even

their opponents acknowledge. A few such leaders
the working classes of this country now have; and
to these real leaders, as well as to themselves, they
owe it to get rid of the petty demagogues and in-
triguers who arrogate to themselves the title of
leaders of the people, and profess to speak in their
name.

It has been suggested that the labouring classes
should return members of their own body to the
House of Commons; but this advice, though good
in itself, is more easily given than carried out. There
are many working men who are thoroughly competent to fulfil all the duties of a member of parliament, — men of good natural abilities, who have
educated themselves and studied politics, more especially in reference to the position of their own
class. But the men of this type are comparatively
little known; though, as they do not take the all-
perfect view of the working man, it is doubtful
whether in any case they would be supported by
that very numerous section of the working classes
who have been politically demoralised by the flat-
teries of some of their so-called friends. The kind
of working men who would at present be most likely

to get into parliament are certain cheeky, ambitious, superficially-clever, and not over-scupulous gentlemen who have taken prominent parts in trade disputes and other trade-union matters. With a little practice these men would make passably-good members; but upon the whole the working classes would perhaps be as well without them. Their knowledge of politics is very limited; and while they really care for the interests of their class, they still regard them as secondary to those of "number one," and they have, moreover, a constitutional tendency to wire-pulling.

The question of sending working men to Parliament has naturally given rise to that of the payment of members, since whatever might be said against the principle of salaried representatives, it must be conceded that payment would be an absolute necessity where working men were concerned. The chief objection to such payment is, that the members would be considered, and would regard themselves, as merely paid servants, having no responsibility and invested with no discretionary powers; and that the fear of losing their situations or offending their masters would predominate over any desire to act independently. It is generally supposed that this would be markedly the case among the working classes, but this, it is demonstrable, is a mistaken view. Working men have already had experience upon this point in the election of paid trade-union delegates; and those who are practically acquainted with the unions know that, though these delegates are either expressly or impliedly pledged to certain broad principles, they have a virtually unlimited discretion in dealing with matters of detail or any unforeseen complications that may arise. In fact, so far as the working classes are in question, there is infinitely greater reason to believe that paid members would, as other descriptions of representatives have frequently done, make tools of them than that they would degrade the members to the position of servants. At present, however, there exists no organisation for raising funds for the payment of working-class M.Ps.; and from this and other reasons it is highly probable that for some years to come the idea of returning working men to Parliament will remain an idea. Working men will have to look outside their own class for their special representatives, and their action in this respect will be the crucial test of the wisdom or unwisdom with

which they use their new power. In the first instance the new masters will probably fail to make
any appreciable alteration in the composition of the
House of Commons; but this will merely be a proof
of lack of experience, not of apathy or want of will.
The power they hold is great and tangible in itself,
and in time they will make it felt, in all probability
for good.

Much more might be said "in this connection"
than there is either occasion or space to say here;
but before concluding, I would just point to one
anomaly in the recent extension of the franchise,
which is curious in itself and affords a good illustration of how little the constitution of the working
classes is understood by those who legislate for them.
The lodger clause of the Reform Bill, while admitting to the franchise a large number of working
men of the type brought in by the reduction of the
household qualification, continued to exclude a large
and important section, whose only chance of enfran-
chisement lay in a lodger franchise, and to whom
any such measure really intended to benefit the
working classes ought to have specially applied.
Among working people, a married man, who with

his family occupies apartments, though technically a lodger, is regarded as virtually a householder. His being a lodger in any sense is a mere accident of locality. The man who in most parts of the country would live in a " self-contained" cottage, must of necessity rent apartments in London and one or two other large places; but he still, for all practical purposes, remains a householder and a member of the householding class, his social position and the calls upon his income being the same whether he is living in apartments or his own house. Lodgers proper, as they are understood among the working classes, are the "single young fellows," the young unmarried men, who do not rent apartments, but are "taken in and done for" at from half-a-crown to three-and-sixpence a-week. This class, which is still outside the electoral pale, is a numerous one, and, if intelligence, education, and independence of position are to be taken as qualifications for the possession of the franchise, one which it is not too much to say is better fitted than any other division of the working classes to be intrusted with it. The opinion of the better-educated portion of the artisan class is now against the early—and, from their position in life, improvi-

dent because early—marriages which were formerly
the rule among mechanics, and thus it comes that a
very large proportion of the unmarried lodgers are
educated artisans. It is generally argued, by way of
apology for excluding the lodger class from the franchise, that a married man with a family depending
upon him has a greater stake in the well-being of
the country than a single man; but the soundness of
this argument is very questionable when it is applied
to the working classes. An unmarried mechanic
earning good wages, and often with a considerable
amount of money invested in banks and societies,
and who is striving to achieve a position of comfort
and respectability, has certainly as great an interest
in the progress and prosperity of the country as a
married labourer who has to support a large family
upon a small income ; and, in point of fitness for
exercising the franchise in a manner calculated to
promote the national progress in which all are interested, the comparatively untrammelled, well-to-do,
and well-educated unmarried mechanic is decidedly
superior to the little-educated, much-harassed married labourer, whose time and mind, if he is a steady
man, are exclusively occupied in aiding in that very

commendable, but in his case often very difficult, domestic operation—making ends meet. I do not mean to say that in the abstract or as a rule an unmarried man among the working classes is in a general sense a *better* man than a married one; but, circumstantially considered in relation to the franchise, the higher portion of the unmarried section are much better qualified to receive and use the franchise than the lower portion of the householding section. In all other matters their superior circumstantial fitness for acting as the representative men of their class is admitted, as is sufficiently testified to by the fact that in trade disputes or any other matter requiring a bold expression of opinion or independence of action upon the part of the working classes, unmarried mechanics are expected to take, and do take, an active and leading part. So long as the franchise was confined to the higher sections of the working classes, the position of the single lodger, though an unjust, was a bearable one; but now the case is materially altered. To suppose that intelligent, well-paid, unmarried mechanics will not consider themselves outraged, and resent their position on finding themselves still voteless, while the franchise is given to poorly-paid married labourers, who perhaps can " scarcely tell a big B from a barn-door," and who, for any want of independence, are always prepared to put forward the same kind of excuse as the Custom-house officer mentioned in Macaulay's *England,* who had fourteen reasons—a wife and thirteen children—for abandoning his prin-ciples to save his place;—to suppose that the unmarried division of working men will not feel themselves ag-grieved under these circumstances, would be to suppose that they were either more or less than men. The injustice of this position, and the ill-feeling which it is calculated to create, are so glaring to any person who understands the working classes, that it is cer-tain to be remedied as soon as the " new masters" have made a right use of their power by returning a moiety of members to the House of Commons who *do* understand their class.

The questions touched upon in this paper, and a host of others forming a veritable political forest of difficulty, are now before the working classes. Through this forest their way will be a long and laborious one. They have most of their wood-craft to learn; the ground is strange to them, they have not selected or been able to test their pioneers, and they will have a strong growth of vested and class interests to cut through. But with patience, perseverance, and self-denial they may make their pathway clear, and in time attain to the utmost good that is to be reached through political power.

THE WORKING CLASSES AND THE CHURCH.

THE relations, or perhaps I should say the non-relations, between the working classes and religious institutions have of late years attracted a great deal of attention in clerical circles. That the classes in question do not attend places of worship in anything like the same proportion to their numbers as do the upper and middle classes, is admitted upon all hands, though it is questionable whether this is the case to so great an extent as is generally supposed. The worshippers of some sects—notably the Primitive Methodists—belong almost exclusively to the working classes, while considerable numbers of these same classes are earnest members of the Roman Catholic and other religions. The Established Church seems to find the least favour among those of the working

classes who do attend places of worship; and it is
probably owing to this circumstance that its ministers have taken a leading part in the recent " movements" in connection with this matter.

Upon the clerical side it generally seems to be
taken for granted that the blame in this question lies
solely with the working classes. " Here," they say,
" are we not merely willing but anxious to lead you
to the church, not for any advantage to ourselves,
save the moral one arising from a sense of duty done,
but for your good, here and hereafter." This, briefly
put, is the church view of the case, and at the first
glance it certainly seems both a just and a kind one ;
but for my own part I never hear this question
broached without being reminded of a little story I
once heard about a German author.   He had written
a work intended to demonstrate a new doctrine in
metaphysics, to the elucidation of which he had devoted many of the best years of his life, and looked
forward to the book revolutionising the philosophical
world.   But, behold, it fell dead, and at length the
author was told by his friends that readers could not
understand the work; whereupon, with a self-practice
of philosophy that does not always go with a profes-

sion of its precepts, he answered, " Ah, well, perhaps the fault is not altogether in the book." Now, with respect to this want of sympathy between the working classes and the Church, I will go a little farther than the German writer, and omitting the qualifying "perhaps," say that the fault is not altogether in the working classes. In this case there are faults on both sides, and I trust that I am not unconsciously swayed by class feeling in believing that the greater fault lies with the Church; though it is only just to its representatives to say that they take wrong views upon some of the chief points of difference solely through ignorance of the modes of life and thought prevailing on the other side. Thus their efforts are primarily founded upon the supposition that because the working classes generally do not attend places of worship, they must in a special degree be an irreligious body. That here the premises to a certain extent justify the conclusion I am quite prepared to admit; but then it is only by confounding the spirit of religion with the formal observance of an outward ceremonial that the premises can be made tenable. On this principle even a ritualist would scarcely attempt to support it, and it can only be from want of thought that ministers of religion argue from it in the way they do.

The classes who do habitually attend places of worship frequently do so from other than religious motives. Dr. Young, of the *Night Thoughts*, perhaps as great an authority upon fashionable religion as could be cited, tells us that

> " Some go to church, proud humbly to repent,
> And come back much more guilty than they went.
> One way they look, another way they steer,
> Pray to the gods, but would have mortals hear ;
> And when their sins they set sincerely down,
> They'll find that their religion has been one."

Again, speaking of the women of his day, he says:

> " Since Sundays have no balls, the well-dressed belle
> Shines in the pew, but smiles to hear of hell,
> And casts an eye of sweet disdain on all
> Who listen less to Collins than St. Paul."

And any change in the matters of fashionable preachers and fashionable church-going that has taken place since Dr. Young's time, has certainly been for the worse. No person with the slightest knowledge of the world—and I take it that even clergymen should have some worldly wisdom—needs to be told that attendance at a place of worship is not necessarily a proof of religious feeling, and yet it is upon the ground of non-attendance that the working classes are stigmatised as irreligious. If, however, we put aside this evidently unreliable criterion, and judge them by the essentials of Christianity, it will be found that the working classes are not irreligious. Brotherly love abounds among them, and those who have the opportunity of seeing with what kindness and self-sacrifice they assist friends or neighbours in distress know that they have that charity that covereth a multitude of sins. To them, living as they do by manual labour, and following more or less dangerous occupations, the import of the text, that in the midst of life we are in death, is more frequently and pointedly brought home than to any other class; and the lesson is not lost upon them. It often "gives them pause," and causes them to think of that here-after, to fit us for which is the professed aim of all religions. And finally, though, compared with other classes, their lot is often a hard one, they do not take those gloomy views either of this life or that which is to come, which seem to be the sole result of some re-ligious beliefs.

To speak of a wide-spread infidelity among the working classes, or of their being *actively* opposed to religion, or religious institutions, is simply to talk nonsense. Such irreligion as does exist among them applies chiefly to mere ceremonials, is passive, and arises from indifference. Unless Archdeacon Sinclair has an idea that such books as the *Shilling Shakespeare,* or the sixpenny edition of Scott's novels, which circulate largely among the better-educated portion of the working classes, or one or two harmless weekly " organs" of the clap-trap school of politics, which form the staple reading of the less-educated portion of them—unless the reverend gentleman in question believes these to be infidel works, the ocean of infidel literature which he spoke of as circulating among working men exists only in his imagination.

Here and there among working men there will be found some half-educated shallow-minded man who, from having read a few such books as *The Ruins of Empires* and *The Age of Reason,* has come to the conclusion that to profess infidel beliefs marks him out as a bold and original thinker. But such men are exceptional, and are only laughed at by those among whom they live ; and after all their infidelity is of the most harmless character, simply consisting in asking if you really believe that the whale swallowed

Jonah, or pointing to the verbal discrepancies shown in the gospels with regard to the inscription placed on the cross at the crucifixion. Among the more thoughtful portion of the working classes there is certainly a considerable amount of that honest doubt in which they believe with the Laureate there lives more faith than in half the creeds. But these doubts are of a doctrinal not an infidel character, and in entertaining them they are not exceptional.

Nor, indeed, are the working classes by any means so exceptional in their general relations with the Church as the representatives of that institution seem to imagine; and in this circumstance lies the germ of their *soreness* against the Church. It is this that turns their passive indifference towards it into active aversion and contempt. The Church speaks to and of the working classes as a specially ungodly section of society, while the real fact is that they are—and this not from choice, but of necessity—only more open than other classes in their non-attendance at public worship, and in what the unco guid consider their desecration of the Sabbath. The Sunday "outings" of the poor are pointed out and denounced as damnable; while such things as the Sundays at the

Zoo and the Sunday dinners at Richmond and Greenwich are left unchidden. The views of working men upon this phase of the question are so thoroughly and wittily embodied in the late Thomas Love Peacock's verses entitled *Rich and Poor,* that I will venture to quote from them in preference to using weaker words of my own:

> " The poor man's sins are glaring
> In the face of ghostly warning ;
> > He is caught in the fact
> > Of an overt act,
> Buying greens on a Sunday morning.
>
> The rich man's sins are hidden
> In the pomp of wealth and station,
> > And escape the sight
> > Of the children of light,
> Who are wise in their generation.
>
> > *   *   *   *
>
> The rich man is invisible
> In the crowd of his gay society,
> > But the poor man's delight
> > Is a sore in the sight
> And a stench in the nose of piety."

This view seems so self-evident to working men that they are unable to believe that clergymen are not perfectly aware of it. Consequently, when in their special addresses to the poor, preachers, with a surprising want of tact, ignore the rich side of the question, those to whom such discourses are directed regard them as insults to themselves, and a proof of hypocrisy upon the part of those by whom they are delivered.

It is chiefly from this reason that sermons to working men upon the Sunday question are non-effective, while as an institution the Church, which by its action in this matter challenges examination and criticism, acts repellently. By its supporters the Church is set forth as an essentially Christian institution, and its doctrines, as embodied in the Prayer-book, are more or less Christian in tone. But thinking working men—those who will have to be the pioneers in any advance of their class—believe that practically the Established Church of England is an institution of the world and the flesh; and when they see advowsons advertised for sale, and hear of pluralists and political parsons, and of men put into family livings to keep them warm for some member of the family, they are inclined to add, and of the devil also. It may be said that working men do not understand the constitution of the Church; and this is true as regards matters of detail, but it only requires the commonest powers of perception to see that the practice of the Church is grossly at variance with its preaching. The surroundings of life make working men look at things in a practical light, and they will never be brought to believe in the real Christianity of a Church which, with ample revenues, displays the disgraceful spectacle of a bishop with thousands a-year preaching a charity sermon for the benefit of poor clergymen, the said poor clergymen being meanwhile, to use a clerical phrase, the real workers in the vineyard. To this it is often replied that, to attract able men to the Church, you must have prizes in the shape of large salaries and high social positions. This working men can readily understand, but only on the ground that even by its supporters the Church is regarded simply as a money-making profession, the same as the law or medicine. But while maintaining the prize line of argument, the advocates of the Church soar far above the merely professional grounds on which alone it can be consistently sustained. They put the Church forward as a purely Christian institution, divine alike in its inception, mission, and the details of its constitution, forgetting meanwhile that such grounds as these are, if followed to their legitimate conclusion, utterly destructive of the prize argument. By a dexterous manipulation, Scripture can be made to support in the letter many things that are in direct antagonism to the spirit of its teachings; but working men have studied their Bibles to little purpose, if the cleverest of text-twisters can give even an appearance of scriptural justification for such a monstrosity—speaking from a purely apostolic point of view—as a modern bishop of the Established Church of England. The Church's greatest weakness is its own want of conformity between its preaching and its practice. That many of the working clergy are Christians in the highest and purest sense, working men are fully aware, and none can esteem such ministers more highly than they do. But the ministers of this class are very often those "poor clergy" for whose "relief fund" bishops preach charity sermons, and to which (the fund), if I have been rightly informed, wealthy rectors send their cast-off clothing. So that while these true ministers endear themselves personally to those of the working classes with whom they come in contact, their position imbitters those classes against the Church in its corporate capacity.

It may be depended upon that the working classes will never be brought to believe in the purity or earnestness of a Church which leaves many of its best and truest servants to struggle through life on miserably-insufficient incomes, while it passes all kinds of worthless incompetents over their heads to the loaves and fishes at its disposal, simply because the incompetents have political or family influence.

If the prize principle referred to above was honestly carried out, comparatively little could be said against it; but the jobbery, place-hunting, and sinecurism in connection with the patronage of the Church are so notorious, that it is a mere truism to say that the pecuniary prizes in it, though defended on the plea that they are necessary to draw able men into the Church, are not bestowed upon the most able or meritorious of the Church's servants. This is a state of things recognised not only by the opponents of the Church, but by its own truest supporters. Recently I had a correspondence with a clergyman upon the subject of the working classes and the Church. Among other things he sent me a printed copy of *A Lecture Sermon* which he had delivered on behalf of the Curates' Augmentation Fund. In it he dwells upon the necessity of only those who feel a call for it entering the clerical profession, and then goes on to say : " When the call now is so shadowy, undefinable, and indistinct that the prospect of a family living, or the patronage of a friendly dignitary is held to constitute that call, is it to be wondered at that many good men and true say, ' What is a call? Is it fitness, earnestness, strong desire ? Is it holiness, aptitude to teach, learning, study, a costly education ? No ; these are calls to starvation, to penury, or at least unbearable affliction. The true call is influential patronage, wealth to purchase, a brazen importunity, a tide-waiter's vigilance, a timely vote, a useful subservience. These things I am not equal to ; manhood forbids. I have therefore no call. I will be a soldier, a lawyer, a farmer, a doctor, an engineer, or an architect.' And thus the Church suffers. Thus the class of candidates deteriorates."

The clergyman who speaks thus is a true, tried, and admiring servant of the Church, and speaks in sorrow, not in anger, nor, though himself a curate, as a person individually wronged. And when such as he talk in this strain, is it a matter for surprise that others, and especially working men, should regard the Church as a modern Temple of Jerusalem—a house of prayer desecrated by buyers and sellers, and money-changers, who must be cast out from its offices ere it can be purified ?

Thus it is that the Church as an institution is powerless to influence the people; the worldliness and corruption that exist under its wing, and which become hideous hypocrisies when compared with its professed doctrines, act repellently. And while there is nothing in the Church to attract the working classes on purely religious grounds, those social or conventional reasons which are often the sole induce-ments to other classes for attending church do not exist in their case. If a working-man does not at-tend a place of worship from an active feeling of re-ligion, he need not do so from any reasons of caste. It has not become a habit with him, nor is it in any degree essential to his maintenance of a character for *respectability*, that he should be

> " A black-leg saint, a spiritual hedger,
> Who backs his rigid Sabbath, so to speak,
> Against the wicked remnant of the week ;"

while his wife or daughter can sufficiently display

such finery as they can get at market or during a Sunday-afternoon walk.

But while the working classes as a body can only be considered as *not* irreligious by a broad and charitable construction of the spirit of religion, as apart from its set doctrines and formal ceremonials, there are, as I have already incidentally mentioned, many men among them who are actively and truly religious in the ordinary acceptation of the term. For these men the Dissenting sects have the greatest attractions. Their services and ministers are considered simpler and more practical than those of the Church; the ministers are paid with a nearer approach to equality, and have, to a far greater extent than those of the Church, entered their profession from personal predilection, or as they put it, from having " experienced a call."

There are also working men who attend places of worship from hypocritical motives—to curry favour with employers or ingratiate themselves with clergymen who have the power of distributing charity. A few attend Dissenting bodies on this ground; but when it comes to such motives as these, Church pays best, and consequently comes in for the largest share of such pauper-souled worshippers.

All this it may be said is merely an attack upon the Church, but it is only incidentally that it is so. In order that the relations between the working classes and the Church may be properly understood, it is necessary to show exactly in what estimation these classes hold the Church, and in the foregoing remarks I have embodied the views generally obtaining among them. Looking at these views, I think it must be admitted that the working-class indifference to the Church is ascribable less to an irreligious feeling than to a contempt for the desecration of the spirit of religion under the guise of a ceremonial systematisation of it. The Church, as it stands, is emphatically not the Church of the people. They believe that on truly Christian grounds it has no claim to reverence or authority, while as a social institution it is not suited to their necessities. So long as the relative position of the working classes, and the habits of life to which it gives rise, remain as they are, it is probable that no Church, however pure, would in the first instance be able to induce them to habitually attend public worship. But a really apostolic Church—a Church whose servants practised as well as preached the teachings of the great Founder of Christianity—could do an incalculable amount of good among them, could lead them to a higher, purer, more actively-religious life, which would in its turn lead to their becoming sincere observers of the outward forms as well as of the essentials of religion. But the Established Church is not of this kind; and ere it can hope to influence the working classes in any considerable degree it must purify itself—must cease to combine the worship of God with that of Mammon.

I do not wish to go into the details of the incidental question of the disestablishment of the Irish Church; but from what I have said it will be apparent that the working classes would regard the proposed disestablishment (especially if it had been self-sought) as a step in the right direction—an advance towards internal purification. On the other hand, their unfavourable opinion of the Church generally can only be deepened by the spectacle of a bench of bishops grimly fighting against justice and the spirit of the age; not for any point of faith or doctrine, but for the retention of State pay originally granted for a tyrannical and bigoted purpose, and at present chiefly devoted to maintaining sinecurists, and giving an enforced legal existence to an institution which has no spiritual life in it. Such a spectacle as this can only strengthen the opinion among working men that all *really* religious men must look upon the Church as " a thing to shudder at," not support.

TRADE UNIONISM ON ITS TRIAL.

A FAVOURITE phrase in the discussions upon trade unionism is that "the unions are now on their trial." And virtually this is true. They are on their trial before the tribunal of public opinion; and as the decisions of that tribunal are all-powerful for good or evil, the arraigned unions should, if possible, have fair play. In this respect they labour under a serious disadvantage. Those who best understand the case for the defence are the least qualified to put it forward in a popular or "telling" form. They are working men, who literally, and not in the conventional after-dinner sense, are "unaccustomed to public speaking," and they are still more unaccustomed to putting their thoughts into writing. And so, while they know that injustice is being done them, they generally feel themselves incapable of refuting the specious, but still false and misleading, generalisations of those who put the case against them, and who are, for the most part, proficients in the art of making the worse appear the better reason.

With the general public there is no intention to act unjustly towards the unions, but their reasoning with regard to them is the reasoning of fear, and that is invariably, though unconsciously, unjust. The assassinations and other scarcely less monstrous crimes planned by the executive, carried out by members, and connived at by the general body of the Sawgrinders' and Brickmakers' Unions, naturally excited the utmost horror and indignation throughout the country; and with the public mind thus attuned, a number of influential organs opposed to trades' unionism in general struck the note that the two unions in question were only fair specimens of the workings of trades' unions generally. And it is from this altogether unwarrantable generalisation, this tricky special-pleading, that the unions are likely to suffer injustice, now that they are on their trial.

In commenting upon the interview between Mr. Gladstone and a number of trades'-union delegates the *Saturday Review* observed: "Considering that we know what Sheffield trade-regulations come to in practice, it is very superfluous to prove anything about trades' unionism in general. We do, as a matter of fact, know that Mr. Potter's pretty theories, when translated into the ugly vernacular of contemporaneous history, mean murder and arson." And this is the tone which the *Saturday Review* and several other papers have persistently taken throughout the trades'-union question. Now, we know that the law has frequently wronged the innocent, and been made to serve as a cloak and tool to knaves and oppressors, and scarcely a month passes without some specially notorious specimen of justices' justice being brought to light. The reasonable deductions from these circumstances are, that the phases of law under which wrong is done should be amended or extinguished, or the particular magistrate who, from cruelty of disposition or want of sense, has abused the discretion vested in him, should be removed from the commission. But if, instead of this, a man were to say, It is very superfluous to prove anything about the general justice and impartiality of the law; we, as a matter of fact, know that, translated into the ugly vernacular of contemporaneous history, its plausible theories mean wrong to the innocent, cruelty to the unfortunate, and impunity to the guilty. If any man were to say this, he would be justly written down an ass. But when a public writer takes an equally senseless and distorted view upon the subject of trades' unions, I suppose he is not an ass; he is only a *Saturday* reviewer, a gentleman who "fancies himself" at "smart" writing, mistakes impudence for epigram, and Brummagem cynicism for cool reasoning.

The anti-union organs belong to a class that powerfully influences the opinions of those outside the working classes—those whose knowledge of the classes in question is derived solely from "organs," and before whom the unions are on their trial; and owing to this state of affairs many people have been brought to look upon trade unionism as a kind of European Thugism — a Nazareth out of which no good thing can possibly come.

As this view is persistently kept before the public by the class of journals to which I have referred, it is to the interests of all classes that the other side of the question should also occasionally be brought forward, and it is on this ground that I wish to show, not by any hair-splitting arguments, but by incontrovertible facts and figures, that the really representative trade unions are not merely theoretically capable of doing, but actually have done and are doing, great good.

The last issued report of the Amalgamated Society of Engineers, which contains the transactions of the society from December 1866 to December 1867, serves to show what a trade society really is and does. At the date to which the report comes down the society consisted of 33,325 members, who were divided into 313 branches, of which 240 were in England and Wales, 34 in Scotland, 11 in Ireland, 14 in British Colonies, 12 in the United States, 1 in Constantinople, and 1 in Croix, in the north of France. The entrance-fee to the society ranges from 15*s.* to 2*l.* 10*s.*, according to the age of the candidate, and the subscription is one shilling per week so long as members are in employment. The total income for the year amounted to 86,225*l.* 2*s.* 7*d.*; but owing to the unparalleled depression of trade that prevailed throughout the year, even this large sum was not sufficient to meet the expenditure, which came to a grand total of 99,105*l.* 5*s.* 8*d.* The 12,000*l.* odd in excess of income required to make up this sum

was drawn from the reserve fund, which at the end
of the year still showed a balance of 125,263*l.* 2*s.* 7*d.*
The chief items of expenditure sufficiently indicate
the nature of the beneficial functions of the society.
First comes the out-of-work donation, which shows a
total of 58,243*l.* 9*s.* 8½*d.*, distributed under a rule
which provides that any member who shall be thrown
out of work under circumstances satisfactory to the
branch to which he belongs shall receive 10*s.* per
week for fourteen weeks, 7*s.* per week for thirty
weeks, and 6*s.* per week for whatever further period
he may be out of employment.   Being unable to
question the beneficial character of such a provision
as this, the anti-union organs try to make it chime
in with their teachings, by saying, with a great affectation of significance, " O, all this sounds very well,
but out-of-work donation is a very elastic term."
And they imply that in point of fact this donation is
merely an euphemism for payment to men on strike.
This implication, like many of the false generalisations from the same quarter, is all the more dangerous and misleading from having a grain of truth in
it.   Since the great lock-out of 1852 there has been
no strike in the engineering trade that has affected

the trade generally, or any considerable portion of it. Still there have occasionally been disputes affecting individual workmen or single shops, and when, in consequence of such disputes, men have, with the sanction of the club, "come out," either in the way of a strike against the particular shop concerned, or by simply leaving, to seek employment in districts where the point in dispute did not exist, they have, of course, claimed and obtained the out-of-work pay. But these cases are so exceptional, and bear so small a proportion to the whole, that in ordinary times it is not worth while to make a separate item of their cost, though in years when they amount to something considerable—to 10 per cent or upwards, say, of the out-of-work pay—the expenditure under this head is mentioned separately. On an average of years 90 per cent at least of the out-of-work donation is paid to men who are out of employment simply from slackness of trade, and from no cause either directly or indirectly connected with trade disputes. For instance, a large proportion of the out-of-work benefit was last year paid to unemployed members in the east-end of London, who were by this means saved from that utter pauperisation to which many of the

non-union artisans of that unhappy district were reduced.

The sick benefit, which allows 10s. per week for
twenty-six weeks, and 5s. per week for any greater
length of time that he may be ill, to any member
who, through sickness or accident, is unable to follow
his ordinary occupation, came to a total of 15,557l.
18s. 0½d. The superannuation benefit of from 7s. to
9s. per week, paid to members of upwards of fifty
years, who through old age or infirmity are unable
to obtain the ordinary wages of the trade, and who
have been in the society for eighteen or more years,
amounted to 5,982l. 13s. 10d. The funeral benefit,
under which the representatives of a deceased member are entitled to 12l., was 5,282l. 14s. 9d.; and ten
grants of 100l. were, in accordance with one of the
rules of the society, paid to members who were by
accident or disease permanently incapacitated from
working at their trade.

Such were the sums paid away for the specified
benefits of the society, but apart from the general
fund there is a benevolent fund, which is replenished
from time to time—generally about once a year—by
a small levy. From this fund exceptional cases of

distress are relieved, upon the recommendation of the branch to which the distressed member belongs. During the year there were five hundred grants from it, ranging from 7*l.* to 2*l.* each, and coming to a total of 2,249*l.* In the annual report only the names of the relieved members and the sum granted to each are given; but in the various smaller reports, of which the annual one is a digest, the particulars of the case are given, and these details afford painful evidence of the misery to which even the most provident of the working classes are liable to be reduced. Here, for instance, are two cases taken at random from a list of several hundreds: " P. H., who was in reduced circumstances through want of employment, had been out of work fourteen weeks, and sixteen weeks the twelve months previous, had both sickness and death in his family, and from his 7*s.* per week donation benefit he had himself, wife, and six children to support. 6*l.* was granted." " W. T., an aged superannuated member, receiving 8*s.* per week, suffering from rheumatism, and in great distress. 3*l.* was granted. He had two previous grants—4*l.* in June 1862, and 5*l.* in January 1864." In such cases as these the sums which the society grant are given immediately, and " in a lump," and are infinitely more effective than the miserable driblets which parish officials dole out. And as by such grants as these, and their out-of-work and sick pay, the large trade unions annually save thousands from the painful necessity of " troubling the parish," or appealing to private charity, I think it is not too much to say that they are beneficial to society in general, as well as to their members in particular.

It is a very prevalent idea that these societies promote and foster strikes; but this is a mistaken notion. It will invariably be found that the objection of working men to strikes increases in direct proportion to the extent and prosperity of the trade union of which they are members. None know better than do working men that a strike is a terribly dear affair, and where a large sum of money representing their provision for loss of work, or ill health, is concerned, they will be particularly cautious how they risk it. For example, the Amalgamated Society of Engineers is the largest and richest of its class, and it is the most free from trade disputes. For the last fifteen years there has been no important dispute between employers and employed in the trade, and those who have a practical acquaintance with the subject know that the men are prepared to go more than half way to meet the masters in establishing courts of arbitration. The general opinion of the workmen is dead against strikes, and scarcely a month passes in which the executive of the union does not, by mediation, prevent strikes, or refuse to sanction them when proposed by some section of the members who consider they have a grievance that would justify such a step.

The moral to working men of such a report as that from which I have been quoting is, I think, tolerably obvious—namely, that a trades' union, to be as beneficial as it is capable of being, should embrace the various branches of trade that are directly connected in the production of any particular class of goods, that it should extend to all parts of the kingdom in which those trades are carried on, and should combine with its trade purposes the functions of a mutual-assurance society.

The best of trades' unions are, doubtless, faulty. What human institution is not? But the whole of the members of the two or three utterly bad ones

among them do not make up a two-hundredth part
of the general body of the unionists; and it therefore shows a culpable ignorance of his subject, or a
still more culpable want of fairness, when a writer
adopts a collective mode of treatment in dealing
with trades' unions, and speaks as though it were
an understood fact that there was only one type of
union, and that the type of the Sheffield sawgrinders
—the type which seeks to compass bad and dangerous ends by the worst of means.

When the diabolical proceedings of the Sheffield
sawgrinders were first made public, no section of the
community was more horrified and surprised at the
disclosures than were the members of the larger and
better-regulated trades' unions. In common with
other artisans, they knew in a general way that the
" Sheffielders"—that is to say, the men engaged in
the cutlery trade, and more especially the sawgrinders—were a rough, violent lot, with whom few
men of other trades could or would associate. They
knew, too, that these Sheffielders entertained peculiar and altogether unjustifiable and impracticable
notions on the subject of trades' unionism; but they
did not know, had not the slightest idea, that they

deliberately planned and perpetrated murders, and were astonished and horrified to find that such was the case; and though less shocked, they were, if possible, still more surprised to find that these notable unionists expected employers to pay the union arrears of their workmen. With such men as Broadhead, and his too-willing tools and supporters, the general body of trades' unionists have nothing in common, and if, while "on their trial," they are, either by assertion or implication, classed with such men, injustice will be done them. There are unions and unions, and each should be judged by its good or evil deeds; or if a few must be taken as illustrations of the whole, some of the best as well as the worst should be cited, not merely because it is only common fairness that both sides of the question should be placed before the public, but also because the better unions are the most extensive and more largely representative ones.

Taking it that the charges of murder and arson ought in honesty to be confined to two or three morally bad and numerically insignificant unions, the chief accusations against the general body of the unionists are, that they try to limit the number of apprentices an employer shall take; seek to obtain a uniform rate of wages for their members, irrespective of their comparative abilities as workmen; and by refusing to work with non-union men attempt to dictate to masters as to whom they shall employ. Now, the Amalgamated Engineers, the trade society *par excellence*—a society which, as I have shown, numbers over 35,000 members, has branches in France, America, and most of the British colonies, as well as in all parts of the United Kingdom, and has an income of over 80,000*l.* a-year—does *not* attempt to limit the number of apprentices, does *not* seek a uniform rate of wages, and does *not* prevent its members working with non-union men. In the large railway works and other engineering establishments where apprentices are taken without premiums, they are in overwhelming proportion to the journeymen, as compared with the crack manufacturing shops of London and Manchester, where premiums are required. Some of the unionists are working for ten or twelve shillings a week less than others; and in hundreds of shops the union men are working side by side not only with non-unionists, but also with the members of a smaller oppo-

sition society. But the propagators of condemna-
tory generalisations give no heed to such facts as
these. That is all very pretty, they say; but, as a
matter of fact, &c., and they finish off by some al-
lusion to the Sheffield atrocities, and then consider
the diabolical character of all trades' unions as settled.

Akin to this is the practice of pooh-poohing as
sentimental or absurd the protest of the mechanical
unionists against their societies being subjected to
examination with a view to restrictive legislation,
while the unions of the learned professions are left
unquestioned. "What nonsense!" say the pooh-
poohists, in reply to this; "there can be no comparison between the professional and mechanical
unions, and their talking in this strain is the strongest possible proof that could be adduced that they do
not know what they are speaking about."

In an article upon "Legal Etiquette," in the
Fortnightly Review for August 1867, Mr. A. Dicey
refers to a letter of mine, published in the *Pall
Mall Gazette*, in which I argued that the combi-
nations of the learned professions are virtually trades'
unions, and that the union of the legal profession in

particular contained " some of the worst features of the unions of the mechanical trades." Speaking of this letter Mr. Dicey says: " On the one side disputants such as the engineer have argued that the bar is like a trades' union, and have apparently drawn the inference that therefore there is no reason to object to any of the rules of trade societies." That the inference here spoken of has been drawn from the fact of the legal and mechanical unions being substantially identical in principle, action, and effect, I do not doubt; but it was certainly not the inference that I drew. Had I supposed that the similarity in the constitution of the legal and mechanical unions rendered the rules of the latter faultless, I should never have spoken of the former union containing " some of the *worst* features of the mechanical unions." The point of my letter was that, if it came to a question of absolutely untrammelled individual liberty of action in trade pursuits, apart from any consideration of " the greatest good for the greatest number," the learned and mechanical unions were alike faulty and restrictive; and that, such being the case, they should alike be subjected to the investigation of the Trades' Union Commission, since it would be a manifest injustice, and class legislation of the worst type, to apply repressive measures to the mechanical unions while leaving the learned unions in unquestioned possession of monopolising powers which, from the "individual-liberty" point of view, undoubtedly act "in restraint of trade." This I still consider a just proposal, and one worthy of the consideration of all who are interested in such matters; and I would respectfully suggest that some of those M.Ps. who profess to live but for the interests of the working classes should bring in a bill asking for such supplementary powers as would enable the Trades' Union Commissioners to inquire into the constitution of the unions of the learned professions.

Two days after the appearance of the letter to which I refer, " A Barrister" replied to it; and this reply, Mr. Dicey says, " directly traversed every one of the workman's assertions." Now, this was not the case; the " Barrister's" letter was simply a bit of special pleading. I spoke of the legal profession, while he spoke merely of bar rules, thus avoiding a part of the question most damaging to his case, namely, the position of solicitors, on whom I believe some of the most trade-union-like rules of the legal profession more especially bear.

Some time since a letter from " A Solicitor" was published in one of the morning papers pointing out that the number of pupils that a solicitor can take is strictly limited; and I remember upon one occasion being in a provincial county court, when a solicitor publicly protested against the clerk of another solicitor conducting a case. He did not, he said, doubt the man's ability to manage the case, but that, though out of courtesy he had allowed such things to pass unnoticed upon previous occasions, he was resolved, for professional reasons, to put a stop to it, as by the laws of the profession he could and would do so ; and it was only upon an understanding that it was " to be seen to" that he ultimately consented to the clerk's going on with the case. Now, if this solicitor was justified in speaking as he did—and I share a very general belief that he was—here is distinct evidence of the legal profession having the power to limit the number of apprentices taken into the trade, and keep unqualified workmen out of it; and yet any attempt upon the part of working men to act in the same repressive manner in respect to their trades is laid to their charge as a moral, if not a legal crime.

The gist of the barrister's reply to my letter was, that the bar is ruled by " the general sentiment of the profession, which more or less distinctly condemns a variety of things, but which anyone who cares to do so may defy with perfect impunity." And he further stated that " a man might hug attorneys to the end of time, and defend prisoners at the Old Bailey for 6d. apiece, without being interfered with by his Inn." Even the literal truth of these assertions is questionable; but admitting that they were true to the letter, I think it must be obvious that they are worthless as practical arguments. No man with the slightest knowledge of the world requires to be told that a barrister who defended prisoners at the Old Bailey at 6d. apiece would be treated as a social and professional outcast, even if he were not formally disbarred; and while it is quite credible that the "great guns" might safely disregard many of the professional conventionalities, there are few people, I fancy, who will believe that one of the ordinary rank and file could " with perfect impunity" defy "the general sentiment of the pro-

fession" in regard to those things which the said
general sentiment "more or less distinctly condemns."
So far as " A Barrister's" arguments were worth
anything, they applied with greater force to the
mechanical trades than to the legal profession. With
mechanics "the trade" is a mere figure of speech,
while the trades' unions—which in no case embody
the whole of the members of a trade—are simply
practical embodiments of that "general sentiment
which more or less distinctly condemns a variety of
things." And it is entirely to its being an embodi-
ment of the general sentiment of a greater or lesser
proportion of a trade that a trade union owes any
power it may possess for regulating trade matters.
It has no legal power, and that its power of sentiment may be defied is testified to by the fact that in
all large trades there are thousands of non-union men
working for " under wages."

If there are any persons who still have doubts
as to professional and mechanical unions being substantially alike, they have only to read the able and
conclusive article in the *Fortnightly Review* to be
convinced that the union of the legal profession at
least is virtually a trade union. And such being

the case, I must repeat that I think it would be only just to include the professional unions in the inquiry of the Trades' Union Commission.

To imply that all trades' unions are as well organised and conducted as that of the Amalgamated Engineers would be as misleading as it is to class them with the sawgrinders' union. Between the latter union and that of the engineers there are grades, and in considering the unions in this light, it is in their favour to find that the larger they are the more nearly they approach to the best specimen of their kind.

The thoroughly bad unions—those that resort to violence, and have in their constitution a lot of carping regulations, which are as oppressive upon the honest individual workman as they are unjust to employers — are almost invariably small ones, and are controlled by two or three unscrupulous individuals, who live upon them. And it will, as a rule, be found that the worst unions are those of trades in which the men commence to work when they are mere children—as early, perhaps, as seven or eight years of age, and when they are utterly un-educated; or those in which the trade is confined to one town, and the trade and its old exclusive rules and traditions have come down from generation to generation. Such workmen as these are in a great measure bad unionists, because they are in a greater proportion than workmen who have been better educated, or seen more of the world—bad men, ignorant, violent, drunken, and immoral.

Apart from the worst class of unions, there are others that have in their constitution much that is, to say the least of it, questionable. Some of them do try to limit the number of apprentices that a master shall take, do object to their members working with, or employers engaging, non-union workmen, and fix the minimum rate at which their members must work so high, that it comes to little less than a demand for a uniform rate of wages. The two latter practices are altogether indefensible, and the policy which seeks to uphold them is as mistaken and shortsighted as it is unjust. They unwarrantably interfere with individual liberty and the legitimate rights of employers, and they tend to reduce all workmen to a dead level of mediocrity. Amendment upon these points is greatly needed, and should, in the interests of the unionists themselves, as well as of the public at large, be enforced—by legislative enactments if necessary.

With regard to the apprentice question, there is something to be said on both sides. If a larger proportion of apprentices are put to a trade than, looking at its condition and prospects, that trade can be fairly calculated to absorb as journeymen, it will inevitably be overstocked, and all who are engaged in it be made to suffer in consequence. And in cases where workmen are honestly acting on these grounds they are justified in endeavouring to limit the number of apprentices. It may be said that parents will not apprentice their children to an overstocked trade; and so far as it goes, this is quite true. But, then, when the trade *is* overstocked the evil is done; and to prevent overstocking is the aim of workmen, who may see the approach of the evil when parents who are unconnected with the trade do not. In most trades, too, there are a number of Pecksniffian premium farmers who have a special predilection for widows' mites, and against the establishments of these gentry workmen will often warn parents, without, however, trying to dissuade them from putting their sons to "the trade." Still, the Pecksniffs generally manage to secure a goodly number of victims, and though it is an incidental part of a journeyman's duty to teach the apprentices, he does not like to be made a bear-leader and nothing else, and so disputes upon the apprentice question often arise in Pecksniffian shops. However, the question practically lies in a very narrow compass. A master has a perfect right to take as many apprentices as he likes, and can get; while workmen have an equal right to refuse to work in a shop which they believe to be conducted upon a system that tends to unduly depreciate their trade, and to appeal to their fellow-craftsmen, on the ground of common interest, to discountenance such a system.

To the vexed question of piece-work there are also two sides. Employers invariably assert, and the outside public take it for granted, that trade unionists object to piece-work, with a view to having all workmen, whether good or bad, paid alike. But this is not always, or indeed generally, the case. The members of the larger societies do not object to take work by the piece, provided that men jointly engaged upon a piece-work job are all allowed to share in the profits of it in proportion to their day-wages. But all workmen do strongly object, and with bitter reason, to the sub-contracting system that prevails in many trades, a system by which one man, with no other speciality than that of being able to drive other workmen, gets all the profits. This system is not only unjust to workmen, but utterly bad in other respects, and has done more than anything else to destroy the prestige formerly attaching to English workmanship, by introducing a coarse unfinished " O-that'll-do" style of workmanship. Again, piece-work arrangements are, as a rule, only verbal ones, and workmen often do not get fair play. Numbers of large employers make it a rule not to pay more than time and half for piece-work, however much may be made, though they will not pay time and half, or even full time, unless it is made. Even where this rule does not exist, and where the work has been given out at prices which employers know will pay them, they almost invariably break down the workman's prices, if they find him making two or three times his day-wages, though these large earnings may be made in a perfectly legitimate man-ner, by the workmen inventing tools, or arranging a system by which, having a number of the same articles to make, they can get them done with great rapidity. Often, too, when a man has organised such a system, the piece-work is stopped, and the tools and system invented by the workman used to do the job by day-work—a proceeding by which the master profits largely, while the workman gets nothing for his invention; and but too frequently a man loses a good shop through the bickerings to which piece-work gives rise. It is chiefly on these grounds that men, as matters now stand, prefer day- to piece-work, though, under an equitable arrangement, there can be no doubt that piece-work—that is, pay in proportion to the quantity of work done— is the fairest system for all parties concerned; and while, as has been shown, masters are in a great measure responsible for the want of some such equitable system, it is only fair to add that workmen are not altogether blameless in the matter, as they often try to overreach their employers by " scamping" their work, and getting other men who are engaged on day-work to surreptitiously help them with their jobs.

For unions like those of the sawgrinders and brickmakers there is nothing to be said; they are thoroughly bad, and those who in any degree attempt to palliate their conduct exhibit a type of mind unpleasantly akin to that of the members of those unions, and are certainly no friends of the working classes. But the proceedings of these particular societies should not, in common fairness, be used as arguments against trades' unions in general. Among trades' unions generally there is, doubtless, much that is condemnable; but there is also much that is good. They establish and maintain that *esprit de corps* so necessary to the well-being of any body of men; they place the workman upon a comparative equality with the capitalist, and form to him an assurance society against the misfortune to which he is especially liable —being out of work. There is much in them to justify, and indeed necessitate, an enforced amendment in their principles, and a stricter adherence in their practice to their alleged principles. But, considering that they have some good qualities, and looking at the condition of trades in which there are no unions, and what would be likely to be the condition of the working classes generally without some such defensive associations, it is questionable whether all the evil of which they have undoubtedly been guilty could justify a desire to altogether suppress them.

And, bad as the unions are, they are sometimes blamed for crimes of which they are not guilty. Because a trade outrage is committed in a trade in connection with which there is a union, it does not necessarily follow that the union is even morally responsible for it. A man, or the men of some particular workshop, may, " on their own hook," commit an outrage of which the executive and the unionists generally would entirely disapprove. In some instances, too, the misdeeds for which they are responsible are solely the result of the general ignorance of the working classes of even the elements of political economy.

To come back to my text, however, "the unions are on their trial," and the indictment against some of them is a heavy one. But though some are unquestionably bad, even these are not "all evil," and their few, if not good, at any rate mitigating, points should, as well as their many bad ones, be put in evidence; and this, speaking from a practical acquaintance with the subject, I have impartially tried to do.

Part II.

—————

OUR COURT.

Most people have heard or read of the great

> " George Robins of auction renown,
> Who made all his money by knocking things down ;"

the man in whom culminated, and with whom died,
the poetry of auctioneering, and upon whose professional like we have not looked again ; the man whose
strength of mind and powers of imagination enabled
him to describe an open drain as "a splendid, well-
stocked, and strictly preserved fish-pond;" or half
an acre of rusty lawn as "a noble expanse of verdure,"
and in whose "going" there was a bid-inducing power
unknown to the present generation. Black indeed
must have been the property which this famous
knight of the hammer and rostrum could not have
made appear in some respects white ; and his achieve-

ments in picturesquely-heightened descriptions have
become proverbial, and matters of social history. But,
great as were his powers in these matters, I am firmly
persuaded that even George Robins, if he were still
in the flesh, and had been "favoured with instructions
to dispose by public auction" of Lock Court, or, as its
inhabitants prefer to call it, " Our Court," would not
have been capable of describing that property as a
highly, or even a simply, desirable place of residence.
There is an all-pervading air of *un*desirability about
it that would have been too much for the great
Robins himself; it is dirty, dark, narrow, dilapidated,
and undrained; it leads off a street scarcely less
dirty, narrow, and dilapidated; and it is one of the
lowest parts of a decidedly low neighbourhood.

I am a working man—what a gentleman wanting
my vote (if I had one) at election-time, or the chair-
man at the prize-distribution meeting of an industrial
exhibition, would probably call "an intelligent artisan"
—and, like most of my class, have seen some " ups
and downs"—but more especially downs—in life;
and in the course of one of these downs, when I had
to tramp in search of employment, I knew an ex-
tremity of poverty that made me acquainted with

such strange bedfellows as are only to be met with in
twopenny lodging-houses or "casual" wards. But
when my limited income, the absolute necessity of
living within a reasonable distance of the workshop
in which I am employed, and in which I have to
make my appearance not later than six o'clock each
morning, and the exercise by the City and Suburban
Railway Company of the house-destroying powers
granted to them by act of parliament, combined to
make me a dweller in one of the twenty houses that
form our Court, they were the means of making me
acquainted with neighbours to the full as strange—
and undesirable as strange—as any of the bedfellows
with whom tramping and poverty had at one time
made me acquainted. Roughing it, however, while
on tramp, is the natural state of things, and is consequently lightly regarded; and indeed you are at such
times, to a certain extent, "happy, because it can't
last;" but that 1 should, while still able to work, and
at a time when I was in constant employment, and
earning the wages of a first-class mechanic, be compelled to live in such a place as Lock Court, was a
state of things that was never dreamed of in my
philosophy until it was actually brought to pass.

Even when I received formal, but uncompromising, notice that the house in which I lived was, with some forty others, to be taken down at one fell swoop for the extension of the City and Suburban Company's line, the coming event—the inevitable residence in Lock Court—cast no immediate shadow before. True, the district was one of the most densely populated in the metropolis, and I had been hearing, with constantly-increasing frequency during the last two years, that houses were getting dreadfully scarce—of the truthfulness of which statement I had experienced an unpleasantly-practical proof by the rent of the house that I had just received notice to quit having been raised twice during my three years' tenancy of it. Still I thought, as I put it to my wife, "O, you'll soon get a house, Bessie, if you set about it in earnest." But when, at the end of the second of our three weeks' notice, Bessie had, evening after evening, reported that she had been "all about, and couldn't hear of a house for love nor money," except "that one in Lock Court that I told you about, that the people are going out of this week," I began to fully realise the horrors of my position.

However, there was now no time for indulging in

useless complaints or regrets, as workmen were already pulling down the adjoining houses; and so,
having slightly eased my mind by anathematising the
City and Suburban Company and Lock Court, I
agreed with Bessie that the best thing we could do,
under the circumstances, was to secure the house in
that place as a last retreat, as we could get out of
the bargain by paying a week's rent, if anything
better turned up before we were finally obliged to
flit. But despite the most persistent search and inquiry, nothing better did turn up; and so, on the
Saturday on which the notice we had received from
the railway company expired, we reluctantly removed
ourselves and furniture to the unhealthy, disreputable spot, which, in common with its other inhabitants, I have become habituated to speak of—alas
that it should be so!—as " our Court."

The van containing our furniture had scarcely
reached the door of our new house ere it was sur-
rounded by such a mob of ragged, dirty children, of
both sexes, and of from two to twelve years of age, as
it never occurred to me could *all* be the product of
our Court; and as they began to get in the way, and
I noticed some of the elder ones attempting to " what

the wise call convey" some of the lighter articles that became visible in the van as the larger ones were removed, I ordered them to go off to their own place, and play there. Whereupon, a gentleman of surly aspect, and with whose bloated, sodden face neither soap nor razor had been recently acquainted, who had been leaning against the doorpost of the next house, watching the removal of the furniture with a sullen and injured air, explained to me, emphasising his explanation by a number of sanguinary expletives, that the "kids" belonged to the Court, and had as much sanguinary right there as me; and added a statement to the effect that the inhabitants of the Court generally would take sanguinary particular notice that I didn't come the sanguinary genteel over them, if I *had* got a wan-load of furniture. To this harangue, which was loudly cheered by the assembled children, I made no reply, merely congratulating myself upon the circumstance that I was not in the habit of " coming the genteel" over anybody, and resolving that I would have nothing whatever to do with the individual who had addressed me, though circumstances so fell out that I was not able to keep steadfast in this resolve for many hours.

About eleven o'clock at night, and while I was still engaged in putting together and fixing furniture, I was startled by hearing screams and the sound of blows proceeding from the next house; presently the screams changed to half-choked cries of murder, while the heavy thudding sound of blows being struck upon flesh increased. Unable to endure the idea of standing still while what I believed murder was being committed, I threw off the grasp which my wife had laid upon my shoulder, went out, pushed through the crowd gathered round the house from which the cries came, and sending the door open with a vigorous kick, beheld my friend of the morning kneeling upon a woman, whom he was half-strangling with one hand, while he hit her about the head with the other. In an instant I had dragged the cowardly ruffian from the prostrate and partly unconscious woman, and after a short struggle, succeeded in pinning him securely to the wall, and was still holding him in that position, and lecturing him, after the manner of the British sailor who rescues the " poor but virtuous maiden" from the attacks of the " libertine lord," in the melodramas of the Vic., upon his brutal and unmanly conduct, when suddenly I

received a blow on the head which sent me stagger-
ing across the room.   On recovering from the mo-
mentary blindness caused by the blow, I saw that it
had been struck by the lady whom I had just res-
cued; that grateful creature, whose bruised, bleed-
ing, and disfigured countenance presented a perfectly
horrible appearance, having made the first use of her
returning strength and consciousness to arm herself
with the leg of a chair that had been broken in the
scuffle, and attack me from behind.   " What the expletive do *you* mean by coming here interfering?" she
asked, fiercely brandishing her weapon as I faced
round to her.   "He can hammer me if he likes, I
suppose, without a meddling expletive like you a-com-
ing breaking people's doors open."   I replied that for
the future he might hammer her as much and as
often as he liked, so far as I was concerned.   "Very
well, then," she said, pointing with her stick towards
the door; "sling your hook, or yer'll get another
hot un on the nob, as 'll help you on the road a
bit."

Thus admonished, I left the house without attempting remonstrance or parley, and was received
by the crowd outside with jeering yells.   Made wise

by my painful experience upon that occasion, I never again interfered with my neighbour's wife-beating pursuits, though I soon found that he was constantly in the habit of indulging in them, his ill-usage of the wretched woman sometimes continuing for hours at a time, and there is little doubt but that some night he will carry out his oft-repeated threat, to "do for her." Then there will be an inquest and a trial, and witnesses will depose that the prisoner came home the worse for liquor about ten o'clock; that shortly afterwards sounds of blows, and of a heavy body falling about, and cries of murder were heard to issue from the house, and continued with little intermission until shortly after midnight, when all suddenly became quiet for a few minutes, and then the prisoner opened the door and exclaimed: "I've done for the expletive this time."

Something like this will be told by the witnesses; and coroners and judges and juries will express indignation and surprise that men should have heard all this without interfering; but then judges and juries do not live in such places as our Court, and have probably never had their heads broken by any lady under the circumstances I have described.

Wife-beating, so far from exciting the feeling of abhorrence with which it is regarded in decent society, is in our Court looked upon, even by the beaten women, if not exactly as a proper and commendable practice, at least as a very commonplace one, and one which no person of a well-regulated mind would be guilty of interfering with. So far, indeed, as I have been able to gather from their frequent quarrels, the beaten wives care much less for the beatings than for the nature of the transgressions for which such beatings have been administered. Thus, one lady significantly informs the knot of spectators who have been drawn together to witness the settlement of a difference of opinion that has arisen between her and an opposite neighbour on some question in connection with a transaction in pawn-tickets, that if her (the speaker's) husband had thumped her on the previous night, it had not been for getting drunk; to which her spoken-*at* opponent, also speaking to the spectators, replies with equal significance, that she would rather be hammered half-a-dozen times for having a drop too much, than once for going with other men. In connection with the wife-beating practices that prevail in our Court, I have observed that, as often happens in other affairs, those who suffer least make the most noise about them. For instance, when the landlady of the house which represents the "wild Irish" element in the Court comes home drunk (which happens about three evenings a week), and her husband gives her a re-monstrative shaking, such as the majority of the women in the Court would regard as a piece of af-fectionate playfulness, she rushes out of the house, and staggers up and down the Court, howling out: "I'm a murthered woman, I'm a murthered woman!" though the strength of lung and thickness of voice with which she makes this statement unmistakably proclaim, even to those who have not seen her in-flamed countenance and reeling gait, that she is not a "murthered," but simply a drunken woman; a fact that is further confirmed by her asking the neigh-bours—who are making no attempt to interfere with her motions—to allow her to lie down and die at her own door; and shouting through the keyhole of the door: "Good-bye, my childer; yer mother's dying; she's a murthered woman!"

The surprise that I had felt on being informed

that the mob of children that I had seen in it belonged to the Court, soon ceased when I learned
how the houses were tenanted. There were, as I
have already observed, twenty houses in the Court
—ten on each side—and each house consisted of
four small apartments, two upstairs, and two down,
of an average size of eleven feet by ten; and yet in
eighteen of these houses there were two, and in some
instances three, families living, each house having
an average of *at least* ten inhabitants, and every
apartment being used at night as a sleeping-room.
This crowding of two or three families into a
house scarcely large enough for a man and his wife,
while it accounts for the large number of children
in our Court, is also in a great measure responsible,
in conjunction with the general filthiness, for the
circumstance that fever and the parish doctor are
seldom absent from it, and for the frequent presence in it, on matters of business, of some member of the staff of an Economic Funeral Company;
for the idea of a pauper's *burial* is utterly abhorrent
to the minds of the inhabitants of the Court, who
will make the most extraordinary exertions and
sacrifices to save the memory of a deceased rela-

tive, or even neighbour, from this last mark of degradation.

How some of the inhabitants of our Court manage to live is a matter beyond my ken. Most of the men call themselves labourers; but there are a number of them who are never in any regular employment, and who can do very little in the way of "odd jobs" of an honest character, as they do not generally rise till ten or eleven o'clock in the day, are to be seen loafing about street-corners during the afternoon, and in public-houses until a late hour at night. The wives of these men occasionally go out for a day's washing or charing; in the hop-season, the wives and some of the elder children generally get a week or two's "hopping;" and once or twice, when I have gone home to breakfast on a morning following

> " a shiny night,
> In the season of the year,"

I have seen a number of the men drive into the Court in the pony-cart of a costermonger of evil repute, and have marked them hastily and furtively transferring fowls and other farmyard produce from the cart to their houses. But the washing, hopping,

and (I presume) farmyard poaching being only occasional events, hardly account for the support, in a
comparatively extravagant style, of a family consisting of a man and his wife, and five or six children;
for however these families obtain their living, there
is no mystery about the fact that, in their fashion,
they live extravagantly. They indulge in "relishes"
—amongst which a "lacing of rum" almost invariably
figures—at their breakfasts and teas, and have an
abundance of substantial food at all their meals, as
is patent to their neighbours, from its being the
custom of the majority of the dwellers in the Court
to take their meals in fine weather sitting on or just
outside of their door-step. The men, as I have already noticed, spend most of their evenings in public-houses; and the number of pots that potmen take
from their dwelling-houses every morning is something astonishing, as is also the amount of coppers
which their dirty, ragged children have to spend;
and any of these strange labourers would be of
opinion that they were literally "drawing it mild"
if they only smoked an ounce of tobacco in the
twenty-four hours.

But though the means by which some of the in-

habitants of our Court live is a thing which no uninitiated person can understand, there are others
amongst them about whose means of living, or
rather trying to live, there can be no doubt. There
can be no doubt respecting the nature of the employment of these two prematurely aged, careworn
women who occupy a bedroom in the house opposite
to mine, whom, at all hours of the day, I see sitting

> " In unwomanly rags,
> Plying their needle and thread ;"

whom I see still poring over their work by candle-
light when I go to bed at night, and not unfrequently
find still

> " Sewing at once, with a double thread,
> A shroud as well as a shirt,"

when I rise to go to work in the morning. There
can be no doubt as to how they earn the " crust of
bread, and rags," with which they keep body and soul
together; *they* work for the " slop-shops," and are of
the class whose sorrows Hood has immortalised in
the *Song of the Shirt.*

The means by which the consumptive tailor, who
occupies the front apartment on the ground-floor of
the house in which the two needlewomen live, tries

to support himself and his wife and two children, are equally plain.   He has, he tells you, seen better days, and there is that in his manner that testifies to the mournful truth of his statement; but he is at present the slave of "a sweater" to the cheap out-fitters.   His bondage, however, is not destined to last long.   He struggles manfully, and shows the spirit of one who would die in harness; but though the spirit is willing, flesh is weak, and the terrible churchyard cough which racks his attenuated frame at last does its deadly work.   One sultry summer's day, after a long fit of coughing, he falls back in-sensible; and then the parish doctor is sent for, and on arriving at once announces that the poor tailor is " seized with death, but may linger a few days." And now the workboard is converted into a bed, in order that the dying man, who suffers from an ever-present sense of suffocation, may be near the win-dow; and round the open window the dirty, noisy mob of children in the Court persist, despite all remonstrance, in gathering, and howl and fight for the best place from which to gaze in at the man who is " seized with death," and listen to his ravings as he babbles of green fields and other memories associated with his earlier days, mutters technical phrases respecting his employment, or humbly assures the sweater, who is present to his distorted mental vision, that he will be sure to have the work done by Saturday night. For four days and nights he lies on the workboard by the open window, mostly unconscious, and muttering and moaning in a feeble, monotonous manner, but occasionally seized with paroxysms of pain, in which he gives vent to screams that chill the blood of those that hear them, and tries to tear his throat. But on the fifth morning, when I look out of my bedroom-window on rising to go to work, I see that the shutters of the tailor's apartment are closed, and know that his sufferings are over; and my wife, reading the intelligence in my eyes, says, "Poor Johnson's gone, then?" I have no need to reply in the affirmative, as at that instant a woman comes out of the house of death, and seeing me at the window, says, loud enough for my wife to hear, "He's got his release, poor fellow : he went off just after twelve o'clock, and was sensible, and knew his wife and children before he died." When I go home at dinner-time, I find that the two children who have that day been made fatherless are to have dinner with me, my wife having undertaken to "look after them," and make up a bed for them in our house until the funeral of their father has taken place; and at night my wife informs me that the neighbours have been making a subscription to help to pay for the funeral, and that she has given half-a-crown to it, and supposes it is right; and I answer that it *is* right; and then shudderingly ask myself if my coming to live here is only a step towards such a miserable end as this, and once more fervently wish that I could get out of our Court.

There can be no doubt, either, as to the profession of the two showy-dressing young ladies at number 4, who lie a-bed so late a-mornings, and come home in cabs so late at night, accompanied by gentlemen mostly of the seafaring persuasion, and from whose house there frequently proceeds "a sound of revelry by night." There can be no doubt as to how they get their living; but the nature of their calling in no way injures them in the estimation of their neighbours, by whom, indeed, they are rather looked up to, and amongst whom they play the part of ladies Bountiful, being liberal in the bestowal of

cast-off dresses and bonnets; nay, when, as sometimes happens, the seafaring gentlemen stay in their
house during the daytime, they give freely to all
comers of the drink for which the Jacks ashore
" suffer;" and the person who can and does give
drink is, I need hardly say, regarded by the majority
of the inhabitants of our Court as a person to be
respected, despite any trifling moral blemishes there
may be in her character.

The " wild Irish" families who occupy the house
of the landlady of whom mention has been previously made are of the " poor but honest" class,
being hawkers, rag-and-bone collectors, baked-potato
sellers, and the like; and if they do occasionally get
drunk and have faction-fights amongst themselves,
that, as their landlady justly observes, is their affair,
and it doesn't matter to anybody if they "murther"
each other; which, by the way, is a by no means
remote contingency, as pokers and flat-irons are their
favourite weapons, and they have already furnished
several interesting cases to the hospitals.

After the street-vendors of tea and breakfast
relishes, the potmen of neighbouring public-houses,
and the parish doctor, the most frequent visitors to

our Court are tallymen. This by no means respected class of tradesmen are said to realise an enormous profit upon their sales; but however this may be in a general way, they certainly get much more traffic than profit in our Court. No one individual ever keeps the Court long in his rounds; but the force of competition, or a spirit of recklessness, always induces some new man to try his fortune in it; and for a time each fresh adventurer is heartily welcomed, and favoured with liberal orders, until he begins to ask for money, when he is at once put down as a most unwelcome visitor, and one to be at all times received with a "not at home," which is carried out by the following "strategic movement:" As the children of the Court are not sent to school, there are always a number of them playing about; and being brought up in the way that they are likely to go, they are early instructed to combine business with pleasure by keeping a sharp look-out for the tallyman while they are at play, and giving timely notice of his approach. By this means an alarm is given whenever a tallyman, who is immediately recognised by his parcel, comes in sight. Doors are then instantly shut, silence is proclaimed, and scouts

are stationed at bedroom-windows on both sides of
the Court. By the time these dispositions for the
reception of the invader have been made, he will
have arrived at the door of one of his debtors, and
sounded a summons upon it. To this call to a
parley there is of course no reply from the garrison,
and a louder, more prolonged summons, with something of a threat in it, is then given. Should it
happen that those next door to the attacked house
are not indebted to that particular tallyman, they
will come out and gravely tell that plundered individual that "There's no one at home there, sir;" a
piece of intelligence which he receives with an evident air of disbelief, but with which he is never-
theless obliged to be content, as there is no appearance of life about the house to contradict the statement. But, as a rule, it is not convenient for any
of the inhabitants of our Court to hold any discourse
whatever with a tallyman who is in search of money;
and in this case he is just allowed to knock at the
door until he is tired, and raises the siege, when his
retreat is signalled to the garrison by the scout at
the opposite bedroom-window; but it is not until one
of the children, who has been "told off" to follow

up the retreat, and see that it is not a feigned one, has returned from his mission, that the lately besieged parties venture out. Soon after I went to reside in our Court, a tallyman who had been unable to get his money served two of my neighbours with County-court summonses; but through some legal informality which the judge discovered in the proceedings, he lost his case. There was great rejoicing and health-drinking in the Court to celebrate this signal victory; and a knot of the women who were discussing the matter, unable to contain themselves, stopped me as I was going home to tea to relate to me the joyful tale of their—for they all identified themselves with the triumph—having had a law-job with a sanguinary tallyman, and licked him; and then they fell to disparaging tallymen generally; and one lady related another case of triumph over one of the hated race, in which she had borne a distinguished part. The man had supplied her with a shawl, and had then been unreasonable enough to want payment for it, and had come bothering her two or three times a-week for the money. Failing to get it by these means, he had thought to "fix" her by calling one day when her husband was at his dinner ; but he had utterly miscalculated the effects of this manœuvre. The husband, being a genius, instantly saw in the visit of the tallyman "a new way to pay old debts;" for, affecting to have then heard of the matter for the first time, and swearing that his visitor must have induced his wife to buy goods for which she had no use, he sprang to his feet, knife in hand, and threatening to "do for him," sent the dismayed tallyman flying from the house, to which he never returned. This story was received with murmurs of approval and applause; and at its conclusion

"We all agreed, a nobler deed
Was never done before."

Occasionally, the owner of our Court is barricaded out in the same way as the tallymen, and he often finds it a difficult matter to eject any of his tenants who do not pay their rents, as there is seldom furniture enough in any house to defray the expenses of a distress. This same scarcity of furniture gives rise to a great deal of borrowing, more especially of cooking-utensils, and, as a natural consequence, to a great number of quarrels between the women, respecting refusals to lend articles, or failures to return them when borrowed; and these contests, which are conducted in a style that would do credit to Billingsgate, frequently terminate in a pugilistic encounter; the noise, too, of the children running about screaming, howling, and, even when scarcely able to speak, blaspheming, keeps the Court in an uproar during the day; while night is made hideous in it by wife-beating, the return home of drunken men and women, occasional midnight flittings, and the incessant barking of a number of dogs chained up in the house of a gentleman who follows the profession of a dog-fighter and trainer.

By night and by day, and considered from any or every point of view, our Court is certainly a most undesirable place of residence—a place of so pitchy a nature, that few may come in contact with it without being in some way defiled; a place where crime and misery jostle each other, and disease is rife; a place in which any latent disposition to depravity and vice, in either man or woman, will be fostered and developed, and where childhood must be well guarded indeed if it be not corrupted. Yet, with all these drawbacks, a residence in it has not the single advantage which it might naturally be expected to offer—of cheapness, for the rent of a house in our Court is six-and-sixpence a-week; though of the four apartments of which the house consists, not one, as I have ascertained by actual measurement,* gives the *least* air-space consistent with health—eight hundred cubic feet, which, according to the highest authorities, is required for the bedroom of a single individual. And when, in houses of this kind, four or five, and in some instances as many as seven, persons *live and sleep* in a single apartment, it can be no matter for surprise that " fever revels there," or that decency and morality suffer.

The desire to get out of our Court experienced by myself and wife extends itself even to our little girl, who will often come running home from school, exclaiming, " O mother, I know where there's a house to let; there's T O, *to*, in the window;" but, upon investigation, mother finds either that the T O, *to*, refers to something that is " to be sold by auction," or that the rent of the house—if there is one to let—

---

* " Our Court" is no fancy or coloured sketch. It is substantially and, save in one or two places, where there is a little necessary generalisation, literally true, and it is derived solely from the personal experience of the writer.

is utterly beyond our means; and returns sorrowfully to our Court, our hopes of escape from which are each day growing fainter, as the railways of the metropolis are daily increasing in number and extent, and dwelling-houses decreasing in consequence.

MY CLUB-HOUSE.

———◆———

ALTHOUGH from its nature my club is necessarily select and exclusive, it is anything but a fashionable one; no "loungers" resort to it, no London correspondent or other small-beer chronicler gives gossip or echoes from it; its situation generally smacks more of St. Giles's than St. James's, and a view from its windows is often of the kind to which even distance would scarcely lend enchantment. But notwithstanding its lack of those fashionable elements popularly associated with clubs, my club is both an important and an interesting one. Its members are numbered by tens of thousands, and it is, so to speak, ubiquitous. I can turn it into any part of England, Ireland, Scotland, or Wales; it is open·for me in France, and if I go farther afield—to Australia, New Zealand, Canada, or the United States—it still awaits me with open doors and brotherly welcome. In short, my club is a trade-club, with its club-house multiplied three-hundredfold and upwards; and it is of the club-house of the trade-clubs, as one of the special social institutions of the working classes, rather than of the clubs as they affect the relations between capital and labour, that I now propose to speak.

Wherever a branch of a trade-club is established, there is always a public-house appointed as a club-house, arrangements being entered into with the landlord for providing accommodation in the house for members of the club who may be on tramp, for members who are out of work in that district signing the "vacant book" and receiving their weekly donation there; and one apartment in the house is specially rented as a club-room. The choice of a club-house is a rather important matter. Those who keep the house have, so far as club-affairs are concerned, to deal chiefly with men out of employment; and, though the letter of their relations with these men is strictly defined, we all know that the same actions may be done in essentially different spirits. Among publicans, as among other classes, there are men who

" hold it for a rule
That every man in want is knave or fool ;"

and individuals of this genial persuasion, while eager
enough to obtain the profits accruing to a house from
the business of a trade-club being transacted in it,
are apt to treat tramps and men out of work,
who cannot spend anything "for the good of the
house," with but scant favour, and to do what they
have to do for them in a very ungracious spirit.
Such conduct as this is deeply galling alike to the
men who are immediately affected by it and those
of their fellow-craftsmen who witness it, and is made
doubly exasperating by the fact that its baseness is
in a great measure negative, consisting in impalpable
touches, which, though obvious to the moral per-
ceptions, afford no tangible ground on which to found
a complaint of any breach against the letter of the
law. To avoid a Boniface of this stamp, and select
a house whose landlord or landlady bears the reputation of being "a good sort," is a primary consideration in establishing a club-house, and in this respect
the trades' clubs are usually very fortunate, for, as
a rule, a mechanic, when "hard-up" or "on the
road," experiences no greater kindness than that

which he receives at the hands of the landlords,
landladies, and retainers of his club-houses. That
there are selfish publicans who regard anyone who
enters their house without spending something for
the good of it as their personal enemy, and who are
utterly regardless of the misery to wives and children that may ensue from the reckless spending of
money for the said " good of the house," I have
pointed out above. I am also aware that intoxicating
drinks have been productive of much evil among the
working classes; but still I must say, speaking from
an extensive experience of the manufacturing districts, that the publicans in those districts, taken as
a class, are not the heartless social vampires, gorging
and fattening on the misery and ruin of mankind,
which some teetotallers represent them to be. In
such towns as Manchester and Birmingham there is
no class of tradesmen which does more of out-of-the-
way trade for the working classes than publicans.
In such towns as these, artisans and others are in the
habit of taking their meals in public-houses; and in
times of dull trade it is a common practice with the
proprietors of these houses to turn the remains of
joints and other broken meat to account by making

large quantities of soup, which they distribute, in conjunction with "hunches" of bread, among the workmen's families in the neighbourhood ; and I have known many families who, when their money-earning members have been out of employment, have derived no inconsiderable portion of their support from such sources. During the last winter, when terribly severe weather was added to the other phases of the appalling distress at that time, and with very little mitigation still existing among the working population of the east of London, none were kinder to the unfortunate operatives than the publicans of the district. In most of the club-houses, and at several other "publics," large well-warmed rooms were placed at the disposal of the unemployed men, who were not only not expected to spend anything, but had often both meat and drink given them by the landlords of the houses. And there are hundreds of men who, when on tramp, have been indebted for preservation from sickness, and possibly from death by the roadside, to the kindness they have received at the hands of publicans, and more especially those at whose houses the business of trade-clubs is transacted. I am no frequenter of public-houses or admirer of drinking practices, and if I thought the extinction of the publican's profession would lead to the suppression of drunkenness, I would be an advocate for such extinction; but I do not believe it would have that desirable effect, and, in the mean time, though publicans may be sinners in many respects, I do not think that any special lack of charity is one of their besetting sins.

The ordinary formal business transactions of a trade-club are of course carried on in the club-room proper. I am aware that some very melodramatic ideas are abroad respecting the proceedings that take place in the club-rooms of trade unions. There are gentlemen who are fully persuaded that all trade unions are virtually Vehmic tribunals, in whose assemblies secret judgments against life and property are recorded, and agents appointed, by lot or otherwise, to put these judgments in force. These ideas were doubtless originally " founded on fact ;" such scenes as the club-room scenes depicted in *Mary Barton* and the drama (constructed from the novel) of *The Long Strike* were probably enacted in real life a generation ago ; and from the investigations of the Trades' Union Commission it would appear that

in very recent times proceedings the reverse of commendable have taken place in some of the Sheffield
unions; but these latter are admittedly exceptional
instances, applying to very limited numbers of men;
and none have been more surprised at the revelations
in connection with them than the members of the
larger and better-organised trade unions, who, Lord
bless you, sir! have no melodramatic stories of this
kind to tell. The usual business of a club-night
is of a very simple, not to say prosaic, character, and
consists in paying and signing for the contributions
of members, making out and signing orders and
receipts, posting-up the books, and proposing and
electing candidates for admission. Sometimes these
proceedings are diversified by a semi-judicial inquiry
into some such matter as whether the circumstances
under which a member is claiming the benefits of
the union are such as justly entitle him to them, or
the discussion of a proposal for giving something
over the stipulated benefits to some specially-dis-
tressed member—a proposal that is almost invariably
met either by a private subscription or a grant from
the general funds of the society. Matters pertaining
to the relations between employers and employed in

the trade are of course also occasionally discussed. If the point under discussion is one on which the feeling of the trade is unanimous, it is speedily settled —so far as the club-room discussion of it is concerned —by the passing of resolutions bearing upon it; but if, as often happens, a difference of opinion exists among the members, the matter is argued out in full parliamentary form, the president fulfilling the function of speaker, and being in a position to restrain unparliamentary language from either party by an exercise of the discretionary fining powers invested in him. On such occasions as presentations and anniversary dinners in connection with "the trade," the club-room is converted into a banqueting-hall— feast, song, and speech-making taking the place of business, and the toast-master superseding the president; and a celebration of this kind is the nearest approach to stage effect that is now to be witnessed in trade club-rooms.

On descending from the club-room, those of the members who are not teetotallers generally turn into some of the lower apartments, and over a social pipe or glass discuss the news of the day, or any current topic of local or personal interest. Here they are often joined by men from other branches of the club and non-unionist members of the trade, who drop in for a gossip, or perhaps on the "spec" of seeing or hearing news of some old mate. If any of the craft who are "on the road" happen to be putting up in the house, they are invited to join the circle, which their conversation concerning their travels in search of employment, and those whom they have met during those travels, considerably enlivens. As they mention town after town through which they have passed, some member of the circle asks if they have seen Bill or Jack So-and-so in this or that town. If they reply in the affirmative, the interrogator goes on to ask how the person in question is looking, and what he is doing; and being enlightened upon these points, probably informs the company that he has formerly "worked mates" with the man about whom he is making inquiries, and then favours them with some reminiscence illustrative of the said former mate being a "rum nut," or "good sort," or having some other special characteristic. This naturally gives rise to the recital of other anecdotes illustrative of peculiarities in the characters of ancient or present mates of other men present, or of individuals known by reputation throughout the trade; these in their turn give rise to other topics, and so the conversational ball is kept rolling pleasantly until the time for breaking-up arrives.

Trade-union club-houses find great favour in the eyes of the professional begging-tramps, as in them they can generally ply their trade successfully. The clubmen to whom they appeal may have grave doubts as to their real character, their glibly-told tale and artistic get-up notwithstanding; but many of them have themselves known what it is to be hard-up, and a greater or lesser number of them almost invariably give the unknown tramp the benefit of the doubt— and a few coppers—thinking, and perhaps rightly, that it is better to be "had" sometimes than from over-suspicion to refuse such help as it is in your power to give to a case that may be one of real distress.

To mechanics belonging to the union, and travelling in search of employment, the club-house is a most valuable institution. In it they can always be sure of a clean and comfortable bed, of reliable official information as to the state of trade and prospects of obtaining employment in the district, and of a kindly welcome and friendly service from their brother craftsmen who use the house. In London, and some of the larger manufacturing towns, there will sometimes be as many as a dozen or fifteen tramps staying in a club-house at one time. A majority of them are generally young fellows who have come up from the smaller provincial towns on completing their apprenticeship; but there is usually one old hand versed in the economies of tramping among them, and he is appointed treasurer, market-man, and cook to the general body. And though the work attached to these offices is considerable, and the profits none at all, the old hands always accept them cheerfully, and perform the duties attached to them in a manner that greatly benefits their less-experienced fellows; for with the money which only enables young fellows when " finding themselves" to live upon bread-and-cheese, they can provide savoury, plentiful, and varied joint-stock meals.

Considered in its social aspects, the club-house of the trade union is a most important and interesting institution, and is emphatically *the* club of the working classes proper. It is a centre of communication both personal and by correspondence; it affords a ready vehicle for social intercourse and re-unions; and in this present age, when, owing to the changes and fluctuations in trade, large bodies of mechanics are constantly flitting from town to town, it affords comforts and a means of economy to working men of the value of which only those who have benefited by their existence can realise the full extent.

PAY-DAY.

IF a young fellow is in love, and his opportunities for courting in a great measure limited to "Susan's Sunday out," he will be prepared to exclaim, with the lover of " Sally in our alley :"

> " Of all the days that's in the week
> I dearly love but one day,
> And that's the day that comes between
> The Saturday and Monday."

With him the extreme preference for Sunday above all other days is a natural as well as a prettily senti-mental one, and to all others to whom it is a day of rest and quiet Sunday is also a red-letter day in the calendar. At a first glance the advantages to a work-ing man of the Sunday, as compared with all other days, would appear to be self-evidently indisputable ; but if the question of the respective merits of the various days of the week was fairly weighed it is probable that a majority of working men would,

after due consideration, be inclined to paraphrase the
old song, and say:

> " Of all the days that's in the week
> I dearly love but *pay*-day."

Saturday with its half-holiday, and Sunday with
its total cessation from toil, and opportunities for
social intercourse, have each its charms, but they are
of secondary importance compared with pay-day.
" O, well, never mind—it all brings pay-day," is the
philosophical reflection with which a working man
consoles himself when put upon some particularly
hard or disagreeable piece of work; and even when,
from having a natural predilection for his trade, the
mechanic's daily work becomes to him in some degree a labour of love, the prospect of pay-day is still
the chief material incitement to labour. The influences of pay-day permeate in a greater or lesser
degree through every transaction of a working man's
life. His social, domestic, and provident arrangements hinge upon it, and his " time bargains" are
regulated by it. If he borrows, it is till pay-day; if
he lends, it is on one and till another pay-day; many
of his more important purchases are deferred till pay-
day; and his arrangements for holidays and other

things involving extra, and not absolutely necessary, expense are seldom finally decided until he sees what sort of a pay-day the coming one will be, for the pay of a working man, even when he is in employment, is not always the same in amount. He may have lost a morning quarter or two from over-sleeping himself, or a day from ill-health or some other un-avoidable cause; or he may have been compelled to " stand off" during a portion of the week through bad weather, breaks-down of machinery, unantici-pated absence of mates, and other like causes. On the other hand, he may have been engaged upon pro-fitable piece-work, or making over-time; so that the actual amount of a week's pay may fluctuate consider-ably, and provisional arrangements depending upon this circumstance have to be ordered accordingly.

The all-pervading manner in which pay-day and its customs and influences act and react upon the various phases of the life of the working classes can-not be illustrated in detail within the space to which this paper must necessarily be limited, and so I will content myself with pointing to some of its more general and salient features. In the majority of workshops employing any considerable number of

" hands," the workmen are paid weekly, but in some
large establishments fortnightly pays are the rule.
To this latter mode of payment working men's wives,
as well as the men themselves, have great objections.
Such objections will to the uninitiated appear cap-
tious and unreasonable; it will be said that, As you
receive precisely the same amount in one fortnightly
as in two weekly pays, it matters not in which of the
two ways you draw your wages; and as an arith-
metical proposition this is, of course, incontrovertible.
But, as a matter of fact, those who are affected by it
will tell you there is a tangible difference for the
worse in fortnightly as compared with weekly payment of wages. Even those who feel this most and
understand it best would find it difficult to explain
how or why this is so; they only know that such is
the case. And here it may be observed that the
difficulty of making it apparent to outsiders that what
to them appear to be mere differences of name or
manner are matters of material import to working
men, is a prolific cause of disputes between employer
and employed. A demand which really involves a substantial consequence to the workman making it will
often appear vexatious and dictatorial to those unac-

quainted with the inner life of the working classes.
In respect to these fortnightly pays, the women will
tell you that somehow or other they cannot make the
money go so far as they can when it is paid weekly;
while the objection of the men to such pays is cha-
racteristically indicated by the fact that they always
speak of the non-pay week as "blank week," and
style the pay Friday—in those establishments in
which, with a view to facilitating the Saturday half-
holiday movement, the workmen are paid on Friday
—"Good Friday." The evils of fortnightly payment of wages are in a general way attributable to
the fact that it is only by receiving their wages at
short intervals that those whose incomes are barely
sufficient to enable them to live "from hand to
mouth" can escape the dire necessity of having to
deal upon credit for the necessaries of life. Articles
of clothing have to be purchased, and rents and other
heavy payments made, on the days immediately succeeding the pay-day, so that towards the end of the
week money generally begins to run short. By good
management, however, and with an early pay-day in
view, a day or two at the end of the week may be got
through with very little money; but when it comes

to this close shaving, "management" may be unable to effect for four successive days what it can do for two, and credit must be sought—then woe is it to the working man. The petty shopkeeper will mark him for his own, and soon have him upon his books; the most outrageous forms of robbery by short weight and adulteration will be ruthlessly inflicted upon him, and in a short time he will be inextricably fettered with poverty and debt. And it is chiefly upon this principle that working men object to the fortnightly system of payment where it still exists.

Some of the most interesting phases of the pay-day naturally occur in the workshop. References to that day are constantly cropping up on the other days of the week. If a shop subscription is being made for some distressed fellow-workman, the observation of the collector is, "You've only to put your name down, you know; pay on pay-day;" or if it is known that other subscription lists have been round during the week, or that the coming pay-day will be a poor one in consequence of its being the one immediately following Christmas, Whitsuntide, or some other holiday, you are perhaps informed that "It'll do the pay-day after next, you know." The youthful speculator who sells pigeons, raffles rabbits, barters penknives and mosaic breast-pins, organises twopenny Derby sweeps, and other matters of that kind among the boys in the shop; and the juvenile fifty-per-cent-er who towards Wednesday or Thursday accommodates those of his fellows, who, having "plunged" on tarts and fruit at the beginning of the week, find themselves in difficulties towards its close, with loans of a penny, to be repaid with a halfpenny interest on the pay-day,—are constantly alluding to and making up their accounts for the pay-day. In the same way, though in a quieter manner, men who may have little money transactions together, or be contemplating some particular purchase, are in a general way wont to make observations in reference to the pay-day while it is yet afar; while men who, in reply to an application for an advance of wages, have been told that "it will be seen to," and new "hands," look forward to pay-day with a special anxiety—the one to see whether the hoped-for rise will be given, the other to see how he is rated.

On the pay-day the important coming event begins to "cast its shadow before" early in the morning. Directly after breakfast the office-boys are

busily employed in bringing in change; and as they
pass through the shop bearing bags of silver or coppers, they are jestingly asked if they "want a mate
on that job," or requested to leave "that lot" with
some speaker who expresses himself willing to take it
for his "little bit;" and later in the day timekeepers
and pay-clerks are passing in and out of the shop to
speak to workmen regarding points on which there is
any uncertainty.

In order to secure rapidity of payment, some properly regulated system of paying, which is understood alike by the workmen and pay-clerks, is adopted
in all establishments employing large numbers of
hands; and immediately upon the ringing of the
bell those whose numbers stand first on the pay-
sheet make all haste to the pay-place, the others
following more leisurely. While the men are waiting their turns, they generally indulge in a little
good-humoured banter. A gentleman who has the
reputation of not being particularly fond of hard
work will be asked if his hand does not tremble;
to which he will probably reply that if it does it is
at having so little to draw; while another, who is
known to "like his beer," will hear "in several

places" that he hasn't got long to be sober now; or it will be said *at* a man who is known to have a weakness for some particular relish that there will soon be a rise in the price of the relish in question; and as those who have received their pay pass out someone who has drawn a good pay will show his money to a mate who has drawn a bad one, and tell him to "look at that, and weep."

On the outgoing side of the pay-window is generally to be seen a small desk, at which are stationed two workmen, who receive money from, and sign cards held by, the other workmen. These two men are the secretary and treasurer of the "Yard Club," and the men making payments to them are the members of the club. (A "Yard Club" is a sick benefit association organised by the workmen of an establishment, and managed by themselves for their own mutual benefit; and in times of sickness its benefits form a valuable addition to the benefits of the trade or friendly societies.) Outside the pay-office all is animation. The men are standing about in knots, counting their money and comparing it with the amounts marked on their pay-notes, as any inaccuracy must be settled with the timekeepers and clerks before they leave the ground.   Standing opposite the doorway is a group, in the centre of which are two men—one holding a paper, and the other with a handful of loose money.   These two are the collectors of a subscription that has been made in the shop during the week; and as subscriber after subscriber comes out of the office he pays the amount of his subscription to the receiver, who calls out the name of the payer, to whose name on the list a " P," indicating payment, is then attached.   Occasionally some man comes out who, not having heard anything of the subscription, asks " Who's this for?" and being informed that " It's for poor Bill Smith, who's been down these three months with a rheumatic fever," says, " O, for Bill, is it? well, put me down for a shilling," and his name is accordingly added to the list.   A noisier group than any of the others is that which surrounds Tommy Jones, who is engaged in collecting the twopences of the members who are in his raffle for a couple of rabbits; while in contrast to these noisy gamesters stands the depressed knot of victims from whom young "Twister" Brown is mercilessly exacting payment of his usurious loans.

The drawing of their wages occasions something of a Jack-ashore spirit among the workmen; and of this the " fishers of men" are aware, and take advantage. Outside the gates of large workshops—especially in the outlying districts of the metropolis—a kind of fair is held on pay-nights. Street merchants of all kinds muster in force, and give energetic utterance to the trade cries in which they proclaim the exceeding excellence and cheapness of their goods. Of these the dealers in "relishes" are in the ascendant, and drive a considerable trade, especially among the boys, many of whom may be seen scampering home carrying red herrings, papers of shrimps, bundles of water-cresses, and other delicacies of a like kind. After the purveyors of cheap relishes come quack doctors, with their " medicated beverages" and wonderful ointments, and dealers in cheap clothes, tools, and second-hand books, who each do a more or less successful trade.

To persons of a sentimental inclination, the eagerness with which working men look forward to pay-day will appear very sordid. But working men cannot afford to indulge in sentiment on this point. With them life is earnest; they must be practical if

they would live; and the practical concerns of their
life hinge in a great measure upon pay. And I have
an idea that hands who work for weekly wages are
not the only persons who look longingly for pay-day.
A big-salaried official or a well-pensioned party, I
have no doubt, looks forward to quarter-day in much
the same spirit as does Susan the slavy, who has to
wait with what patience she may for the arrival of
that day ere she can purchase that bonnet marked at
a sacrificial price on which she has had her eye de-
siringly fixed for weeks previous.

To pay-day, as to most other things, there are
two sides; and while the receiving side of it is pleasant to contemplate, its paying-away phase may be
quite the reverse. The approach of pay-day may be
regarded ruefully when it calls for the payment of a
"little bill" that you do not know how to meet, or
when it involves the settling for a Derby in which
you have "lumped it on" a horse that has run "no-
where." But with things of this kind the working
man has happily no concern; and save for the fact
that the amount of his earnings is often unpleasantly
small, pay-day would be to him a day of unmitigated
pleasure.

A WORKMAN'S MORNING CALL.

When I say that I am a working man—a working man in the general acceptation of the term, and not in that questionable sense in which gentlemen of wealth and position sometimes apply it to themselves when angling for a cheer at a public meeting—I need scarcely add that my morning call is not the formal card-leaving call of fashionable society. No; it is not a fashionable call, for it comes at the very unfashionable hour of half-past five in the morning, and if you happen to live at any considerable distance from your place of employment, even earlier than that; and it is certainly not a formal one, for it is the call to work, and must be obeyed. At one time it comes in the shape of the sharp tapping on your bedroom window of the long wand of the professional caller, at others of a peal on the knocker by the policeman on the beat (in working-class districts the policeman on night-duty often makes a considerable addition to his income by calling workmen) or some mate who, having to go farther than yourself, is giving you a call as he passes; and often it comes in the quieter, but no less emphatic or irresistible, form of a dig in the ribs from your watchful and wakeful wife, who, being chief of the commissariat department, has a vital interest in seeing that the family bread-winner does not lose time and money by "sleeping in." Now, as early rising is supposed to be conducive to the attainment of health, wealth, and wisdom, working men ought of course to regard their morning call as a blessing; but as in their case it is one of that questionable kind of blessings that cannot be avoided—and blessedness is apt to pall when it becomes an every-day affair and is practically compulsory—they do not as a rule regard the early rising which they of necessity practise with that degree of favour that might be supposed by the admirers of proverbial philosophy. Various plans are adopted with a view of mitigating the unpleasantness of this trying call. Some men do not have themselves called till the last minute, when they instantly spring out of bed, dress themselves as rapidly as possible, and hurry off to work without giving themselves a moment's pause for thought. Others like to be called a quarter of an hour before they have to rise, in order that they may have time to get thoroughly awake before turning out; while those who are conscious of a more than ordinary infirmity of purpose in this respect will stipulate with the caller that he is not to be content with the ordinary response of "All right!" called out from the bed, but to stick to his post till he has brought them to the window; or they will even instruct "the missis" to be sure to kick them out should she perceive their own resolution failing them. Each of these plans has its advantages; but after due consideration, and speaking from experience, I think the first is, upon the whole, the best, as this call is one of those things of which it may be emphatically said that the more you think about it the less you like it.

As a novelty, or when it is necessary for some special purpose, early rising is a very fine thing, and your anxiety then is to make sure of being called.

Under the circumstances the Queen of May acts naturally when she says,

> " Call me early, mother dear ;"

as does also Sir Carnaby Jenks, of the Blues, when, having arranged to go and see a " mill" that is to be brought off early in the morning, he instructs his " fellow" to be sure to call him at four; or young Nimrod Smith, when he arranges for an early call, should

> "A southerly wind and a cloudy sky
> Proclaim a hunting morn."

I can well understand people being enthusiastic in respect to early rising under such circumstances as these. Never shall I forget the eagerness and anxiety with which I awaited my own first morning call. That on that all‑eventful morning the policeman who usually called my father would be engaged with burglars, that my father would oversleep himself, and that I should in consequence be allowed to " sleep in" if I depended upon others, were with me foregone conclusions, and so, despite my father's reiterated assurances that it would be " all right," I secretly determined to watch for myself. With this view I betook myself to bed about eight o'clock,—

" 'Twas in the prime of summer time,
An evening calm and cool,"—

thinking to sleep during the earlier watches of the
night, and thus insure watchfulness in the morning. But "the best-laid plans of mice and men
gang aft agee," and so went my well-intentioned
plans in this instance. In vain I tried to count ten
thousand; in vain I turned from side to side and
raised and lowered the pillows; in vain I tightly
closed my eyes and buried my head in the clothes,
and adopted a variety of other means traditionally
supposed to be productive of somnolent effects. The
fear of oversleeping myself was too much for my desire to sleep, and I lay tossing and tumbling until
about midnight, and then, just as I was resolving
that it was by that time too late for me to go to
sleep at all, and that I must now at all hazards keep
awake till it was time to rise, I fell into a feverish,
nightmarish kind of doze. When I awoke it was
daylight, and I instantly became convinced that my
worst fears had been realised, and that I had "slept
in." Acting on the impulse of the moment, I rushed
downstairs to look at the clock, which to my surprise
pointed to twenty minutes to four. "O, it must have

stopped," was the idea that instantly occurred to me. But no ; there it was, ticking away with a regularity and calmness that to my heated imagination seemed intentionally aggravating; and so I returned up-stairs, and, drawing on my trousers—the new "work-ing" moleskins, with the glories of which my mind had been filled for a month past—lay down, intend-ing to wait as patiently as I could for five o'clock. My patience, however, had very little trial, for in a few minutes I was in a sound sleep, from which I was only aroused by the ran-tan of the policeman ; so that it was to the ordinary machinery after all, and not to my own watchfulness, that I was indebted for my first morning call.

Such intense anxiety as this naturally wanes after the first two or three mornings, and though there is for some months a *comparative* novelty about their early rising which deprives it of much of its unplea-santness in the case of boys first starting to work, the majority of them are thoroughly disenchanted after they have had a winter of it. But though boys may soon cease to regard their morning call with absolute pleasure, it generally continues for a year or two to have for them a compensatory advantage. Although when they go to work they are generally supposed to put away childish things, they commonly retain that especial weakness of boyhood known as a "sweet tooth." Their partiality for "relishes" and sweets continues, and indeed is rather increased, as the pocket-money they receive out of their wages enables them to occasionally add, at their own proper discretion, some favourite relish to their breakfast or tea, or to indulge more extensively than they could formerly do in the delectable wares of the cheap confectioner. Now, to a boy with a sweet tooth "the run of the cupboard" is a most desirable thing; and by getting downstairs a few minutes before his father, a boy who is going to work secures this desirable run. He can take a slice off the cold pudding left from yesterday's dinner, spread jam on the bread-and-butter that his mother had left for his morning snack, make up a paper of oatmeal-and-sugar for himself, or, if it is in the fruit season, lay hands on a few apples or pears; and such things as these are to a boy no small compensation even for compulsory rising. If these visitations to the household larder become too heavy, it is sometimes necessary to give the sweet-toothed youth a "caution." This is generally done by mixing cayenne-pepper with the sugar. When the victim to this trap has taken a spoonful of the mixture, he instantly sets up a howl, under the impression that he is poisoned, an impression in which he is confirmed by his parents, who come downstairs on hearing his cries, and explain with simulated horror that, having missed quantities of sugar, and suspecting it to have been taken by the rats, they had put arsenic in the sugar-basin; and it is only when they begin to laugh at his dismay on hearing this piece of intelligence, that it begins to dawn upon the unhappy young lover of stolen sweets that he is merely sold and detected, and not poisoned.

In a climate like ours the weather of course has a material bearing upon the class of morning calls of which I am speaking. In bright summer weather early rising is in a great measure its own reward. True, you are more drowsy in warm than in cold weather; and if the night is very hot, and you are living in one of the close, crowded working-class districts of a manufacturing town, you may not have been able to get to sleep till towards morning, and you consequently awake when called in a very grumbling frame of mind. But this feeling only lasts for the half-sleeping, half-waking minute or two that follows an abrupt and involuntary awakening. When once properly awake, you feel no desire to lie abed in the broad daylight, while there is no fear of a blood-freezing chill to restrain you from turning out. When you get out-of-doors, everything tends to impress you with the idea that on this sort of morning at least early rising is certainly beneficial to health, whatever influence it may have upon wealth and wisdom. Even in the large towns the sky is at this hour clear, and the air comparatively pure, and its bracing freshness is doubly grateful by reason of its contrast to the hot, stifling atmosphere which will necessarily prevail in the workshop as the day advances and the sun attains its meridian power. And then your mates, or gentlemen who are out for a morning stroll,—for there are always numbers of volunteer early-risers in the summer,—holiday-makers on their way to catch early trains, schoolboys going to bathe, and everyone else you meet, are in such good humour under these genial atmospheric influences, and seem so much disposed to give voice to the chorus of Frederick Maccabe's " Early in the morning," that by the time you reach your shop you are in quite a happy frame of mind from the combined effects of the beauty of the morning and the force of sympathy.

But in the winter, and on those raw bleak mornings which figure so abundantly in our springs and autumns, the working man's call is a bore—

"without relief,
Even for the gloss of love to smooth it o'er ;"

for the coaxing "Now, my dear," of your wife in no way reconciles you to it; on the contrary, it rather aggravates your sense of injury than otherwise, as you are inclined to think, and indeed sometimes to say, "O, it's all very well for *you* to talk that way; you can lie still for another couple of hours." And when at last you have screwed your courage to the point of tumbling out, and shiveringly, and amid a volley of yawns, begin to dress yourself, you regard your partner enviously, and gaze on your now vacant place in the bed with an eye which, were there really such a thing as "speaking glances," would certainly say,

"O, bed ! O, bed ! delicious bed !
Thou heaven upon earth to the *sleepy* head !"

wishing in the mean while that it were Sunday morn-

ing. Outside, too, all is cold and dark, and the mood
of those whom you meet partakes more or less of the
aspect of the morning. On these cold dreary mornings the gleam from the hot-coffee stall comes like a
guiding-star through the gloom, and the coffee itself
is as welcome as water in the desert. Here you get
warmth to your hands on the outside of the cup, and
for the inner man from the liquid, which you get
piping hot, for the proprietors of these stalls are
aware that that quality is regarded by their morning
customers before strength or sweetness. If, after you
have been thawed a little by a cup of hot coffee, you
happen to meet some thinly-clad, delicate-looking
factory boy or girl, and find that you have still an
odd copper left in your pocket, you will probably
treat them to a cup; for the necessity for turning
out in the winter mornings is one of the things in
which "a fellow-feeling makes us wondrous kind,"
and the popular belief among working men that a
fellow is never any the poorer for odd coppers spent
in such a way as this, is at any rate a kindly one,
even though political economists of the Alderman-
Cute stamp might be able to demonstrate that it is
not mathematically accurate. The effects of a penny

cup of coffee, however, cannot be expected to last long, and even the best of workshops are chilly and draughty during the early hours of a cold morning; so that in the winter the working man's morning call is upon the whole a decidedly unpleasant affair.

This morning call brings about a rapidity in dressing which would astonish some of the fashion-plate type of swells. In the warm weather, when things are done leisurely, about ten minutes are generally occupied in rising, dressing, getting down-stairs, having "a swill," eating a morning snack, loading a pipe, and getting out of doors. But in the winter all this is done in five minutes; and should a man be pressed for time, he can, by using a little extra despatch, and omitting the snack and pipe, dress and be in the street in two minutes from the time he steps out of bed. In passing through the streets, too, early in the morning, you see " a thing or two" that can only be seen at that hour. You see tramps and the houseless poor creeping out from the holes and corners in which they have been sleeping; and, by way of contrast, you see the votaries of pleasure and "the daughters of the night" turning out from their haunts—sights equally sad and unlovely in their respective ways.

Although in the winter the working man's morning call is a really unpleasant affair, and though on mornings when he happens to be particularly sleepy, or the weather unusually cold, he may in a half-jesting way grumble at it, he knows that it is after all one of the inevitable small ills of life which all meet with in some shape, and regards it accordingly. He knows, too, that while it is only a small evil, it is one out of which great good comes, for so long as he is subject to his morning call, so long is he in work— is in a position to support his wife and children in comfort, and enjoy "the glorious privilege of being independent." And it is only when from sickness or want of employment he is no longer subject to his morning call, that the working man grieves in sad earnestness.

ON THE NIGHT SHIFT.

THERE is, we are told, a time for all things; and nature and custom alike point to night as the time for sleep, the time when work should cease from troubling, and the toilers and spinners be at rest. There is, however, no rule without an exception; and though the majority of mankind are happily in a position to enjoy "tired nature's sweet restorer" in its most fitting and refreshing season, there are many who, in order that the business of life may go on unbrokenly, must perforce " turn night into day," watching and working by night, and sleeping as best they can by day. In the present age night-work is simply an absolute necessity, as without it the machinery of our social life would come to a stop. The furnaces of our iron-manufacturing districts must be fed and watched by night as well as day — must

have their night- as well as day-shift of attendants;
night-cabmen, watchmen, and policemen are scarcely
less necessary than night-forgemen; and it is to the
night-work of editors, printers, clerks, sorters, drivers,
guards, and others connected with newspaper, postal,
and railway work that we are indebted for our daily
papers and morning letters.

Habit, being second nature, will do a great deal
in the way of softening and making bearable things
intrinsically disagreeable, and to the novice seem-
ingly unendurable; but still, when opposed to *first*
nature, habit gets very much the worst of it; and it
being one of the first laws of nature that man should
sleep by night, even habit can never quite reconcile
you to night-work, especially if you are in the tan-
talising position — as is frequently the case when
night-work has to be carried on all the year round
—of taking day- and night-shifts week and week
about.

Abstractly speaking, the night-workers may be
said to be a numerous body; but, compared with the
countless millions who work by day, their numbers
are of course infinitely small — so small that they
cannot be taken into consideration in the general

arrangements of social and domestic life. These
arrangements are naturally planned with a view to
the convenience of the grand majority, a circumstance from which the night-workers are inevitably
material sufferers. As you go to your work you
meet hundreds of other workmen returning from
theirs, and you are almost inclined to believe that
there *must* be something of triumph or derision in
the smile of good-fellowship with which they greet
you. You cannot help reflecting that they will, as a
rule, find a bright, cosy room, a nice warm tea, and a
smiling wife, mother, or landlady waiting for them;
and that by the time you are settling down to your
work they will be comfortably ensconced by their
own fireside, or be " cleaned up" preparatory to
going for " a turn round," or a visit to some reading-
room or place of amusement, or, if they are courting,
for a walk with their sweethearts. These considerations bring it home to you that you are in some sort
a social outcast, to whom all such evening joys as
these are denied, and you are accordingly disposed
to take a gloomy view of your position as you pass
to your work. A little calm reflection, however,
when out of sight of the joyous, home-going multi-

tude, enables you to see that the hardship of your
position in these things is in sentiment, in the "say-
so" of the thing, rather than in fact. Of course, on
nights when some piece that you have a particular
desire to see is being played at the theatre, or anything of a special character in which you have an
interest is coming off, you are inclined to curse the
fate that placed you on the night-shift; but then in
the race-week, and on the days on which any particular out-door demonstration takes place, you have
" the pull" of the day-men; and since Saint Monday has become a tacitly acknowledged institution,
you have the advantage of being in a position
to occasionally join in its worship without loss of
pay.

It is on going home from your work in the morning that the material ills to which your anomalous
position of a night-worker makes you specially heir
begin to fall on you. The day-workers whom you meet
passing to their work, looking blue and cold in the
chill morning air, which they feel with a twofold
severity from having just left their warm bed, certainly regard you with envy, thinking to themselves,
" Ah, he's all right; he'll soon be comfortably fixed

between the sheets." But this circumstance affords you no gratification. You know the ideas of day-men as to what awaits you are all vanity; you know that there will be no

> " Eye to mark your coming,
> And grow brighter when you come."

Womankind are still in bed, and no smiling house-wife will be on the threshold to greet you with that "I've always a welcome for thee" air with which they receive the day-men on *their* return from work. No cheerful fire, no warm tea and toast await *you.* The house is still and gloomy, and in the winter cold and dark also; and as you bark your shins against chairs and tables while groping for the matches, you are inclined to think you are for the time being in

> " A dwelling-place—and yet no habitation ;
> A house—but under some prodigious ban
> Of excommunication."

If the noise of your entrance happens to wake "the missis," you are perhaps greeted with a sleepy "Is that you, Jack?" and are informed that there are some sticks in the oven if you like to make yourself a cup of coffee; but you don't care about making yourself coffee, and so you wash and hasten to bed. You are just about to "drop off" when the female population begins to turn out, and sleep, so far as you are concerned, is more or less effectually murdered. Fire-grates are poked out, brooms and buckets whisked about, and breakfast-things laid with a clatter that to you seems perfectly infernal. Then come the milkmen, and the retail purveyors of watercresses, red herrings, and the other breakfast delicacies more particularly affected in working-class neighbourhoods, making morning hideous to you by their stentorian cries. After breakfast such of the children of the neighbourhood as are not at school begin to play about, a proceeding which gives rise to no small noise, and about noon the inevitable organ-grinder puts in an appearance. This varied and ceaseless clamour either keeps you altogether awake, or makes your sleep direly dreamful, snatchy, and unrefreshing, nor have you any remedy against such disturbing influences. If you complain, everybody is (conventionally) very sorry; "but still," you are told, "housework must be done, you know; and of course you can't expect hawkers to stop their trade or children to be penned-up in the house, just to suit *you;*" and being unable to controvert these truisms, it only remains for you to suffer and be strong. Thus it will be seen that so far as the important matter of sleep is concerned, those who are compelled to "turn night into day" are considerable sufferers by the transposition; and even in the afternoon, when you come downstairs to your late dinner or early tea, you cannot help feeling that your presence in the house at that hour is in some sort an unwarrantable, even though an involuntary, intrusion on "the wife's dominion"—cannot help feeling, in a word, that you are in the way.

When actually at work things are not quite so bad; for though you never feel thoroughly at home with your work at night, and do not get on as smoothly and satisfactorily with it by gas or candle light as by daylight, you have that broad general kind of consolation embodied in the Tupper-like saying, that work is only work after all, whenever it has to be done.

Of the various industrial hives in which the work must go on by night as well as day, and in which there are consequently night-shifts of hands engaged, railway steam-sheds afford perhaps the best general illustration of night-work and workers; and it was in one of these that the present writer had his experience of being on the night shift. On reaching the shed, the first proceeding of all hands was to place their "bagging" (the food for their supper, and the meal that answers to the dinner of the day-workers) in some safe and clean place; and this accomplished, we would pitch into our work with a view to getting it as forward as possible by the supper-hour, in order that we might linger over that meal a little beyond the specified time; for supper-time is the brightest oasis in the desert of night-work. At that time the large doors through which the engines come in were closed, temporary screens were erected around the stove as a protection against the fierce draughts that usually prevail in a steam-shed, seats were laid; and these preparations completed, supper commenced, and cooking, eating, and yarn-spinning became the order of the night. This latter was a rather important feature in our proceedings; for as we glanced out into the surrounding darkness, and remembered that we had still to work on through the watches of the night, a camp-fire-like feeling would fall upon our circle, and a good yarn would have for us that added charm which it has for a company of prairie-hunters, or the seamen of a midnight watch. This feeling is experienced with a twofold intensity at " the noon of night," about which time men on the night shift generally take their second meal; and sometimes the stories told at this witching hour are of a character calculated to make the younger boys subsequently raise objections to being sent alone into any dark corner of the shed.

There is always plenty of fire in and about a steam-shed, a fact of which tramps and others who have not where to lay their heads are aware, and of which they frequently take advantage. Seeing a strange figure moving about in the light of the large grate containing the " live" coals used for getting up steam, you go out, and find some hungry, footsore, wayworn tramp, who apologises for his presence, and hopes " the hands" will let him lie down by the fire. But the hands *won't.* " Lie down by the fire, be blowed!" they say; " come on into the shed, and have a bit of something to eat, and then we'll find you a better place than that to lie down in;" and so saying they take him in, and having seated him by the stove, assail him with invitations to " Have a bit of supper with me, mate." Having complied with as many of these invitations as he is able, a bed of planks and sacking is made up for him in some snug corner, and he is soon sleeping the sleep of the weary. To share his "bagging" with some houseless wanderer is an ordinary occurrence with a man on the night shift ; but in these cases the blessing of the widow's cruse seems to be given to the food, for notwith-standing that night-work sharpens the appetite, a supper thus shared seems no less satisfying than those that have suffered no division, even though the better half of it has been given to your chance companion.

Sights and sounds that seem commonplace by day appear strange and striking by night. In the day-time heavy goods and fast specials pass alike un-heeded ; but there is something weird and solemn in the sound of an approaching train when it comes borne through the stillness of the night, now faintly heard as it is intercepted by some intervening curve, presently coming loud and clattering as it again gets into the line of hearing, then heavy and boom-ing as it passes through some deep cutting, and

finally thundering and crashing as it rolls by and
passes away into the far distance, sending back its
varied sounds in a manner that reminds you of a pi-
broch played on a march through some mountain
gorge.   After the " through goods," perhaps, comes
the fiery wi-sh-sh of the night mail north; and though
you have seen it scores of times before, you are again
tempted to rush out to get a glance of it as it flashes
past :

" Forward and northward ! fierce and fleet,
    Through the mist and the dark and the driving sleet,
       As if life and death were in it ;"

the faces of the passengers, of whom you sometimes
get a glimpse in the dim lamplight of the carriage,
looking ghost-like as they flit by.   Such things as
these, and the pleasant breaks afforded by the meal-
hours, do much to relieve the monotony of night-
work, and though sometimes the hours seem to go
slowly, the longest of winter nights comes duly to a
close.

By way of a change you may occasionally go for
a short " turn round" in your meal-times.   At supper-
time you meet the day-men returning from their
evening stroll, and hear the latest "tips" as to what

has been going on in town; and in what, for want of a more expressive term, you call your dinner-hour, you see various phases of the night-life of the streets. Besides the night-workers, there are always flitting about numbers of more or less voluntary night-birds. At an hour when those who have to turn out early in the morning are already in their first sleep, the streets are still in a state of comparative bustle with the passing to and fro of the audiences discharged from the theatres and other places of amusement. Then follows the turning out of the " die-hards," who have remained in the public-houses till closing time. These individuals are generally given to making night hideous as they stagger or are led home, and the same may be remarked of those gentlemen who have been supping not wisely but too well, who also come to the fore about this time; and of the fast youths who turn out from the "hops" and night-houses in the small hours of the morning. And during these same small hours Mr. Bill Sykes is occasionally to be seen furtively passing on his way, on professional purpose bent. These waifs and strays, who love the darkness rather than the light because their deeds are evil, are by many persons regarded as the most attractive features of the night life of cities. But though they certainly afford much food for reflection, both to the philosophically and sensationally inclined, it is questionable if, after all, their sayings and doings have as much true interest in them as have those of the honest night-workers.

SATURDAY TRADING.

Saturday is, for a variety of reasons, any one of which would be sufficient to make it a red-letter day in the weekly calendar, the brightest and best of "week-days" to working men. To many of them it is now a half-holiday; and to a still larger number who do not enjoy the Saturday half-holiday proper it is a comparatively short working-day, as on it they "knock-off" at four o'clock instead of at six, as on other working-days of the week, and are thus in a position to get through with—by an hour that still leaves them time for a "stroll round town" or a visit to a place of amusement, on this the only night on which they can venture to stay out a little later than usual without any evil resulting from their "sleeping-in" on the following morning—those odd household jobs which, being more in the mechanical than the purely domestic line, are set aside to be done by "father," and are allowed to stand over and accumulate—especially in the winter months—until Saturday afternoon, when father "tackles" them immediately upon coming home, with a view to finishing them while still in his working clothes. For even odd jobs involve wear and tear of clothing, and are not to be rashly "tackled" by working men when they have once assumed their Sunday, or even "second-best" suits. And by all working men—even by those who, from the nature of their employment, are "bound to the wheel" longer and more closely on that day than on any other—Saturday is looked forward to with feelings of pleasure as the day that marks the close of the weekly round of labour, and as being the harbinger of that one day of the seven which is to working men literally a day of rest, but on which, while they *do* rest and *are* thankful, they are by no means torpidly idle. No one knows better than they do that

> " Absence of occupation is not rest ;
> A mind quite vacant is a mind distress'd."

In reading, taking their walks abroad, and, in their degree, exchanging those social courtesies and hospitalities which their mode of life prevents them from observing upon other days, the bulk of the working classes on their day of rest find that diversity of occupation which, when self-sought and selected, is the truest and most invigorating kind of rest to the habitual worker, and which in their case has also a refining effect upon their character, and gives a little pleasant, beneficial, and much-needed variety to their round of life. But the brightest feature of the Saturday—the feature on which depends many of the most important and interesting customs of the day, and which in a greater degree than all the others gives a distinct and characteristic tone to the day— consists in the fact that it is pay-day, the day on which the working man draws his weekly wages; and being thus, after his kind, flush of money, is, like other men under the same circumstances, elevated in spirits in consequence, even though, as he will sometimes himself observe, with an affectation of woe, he has only the pleasure of carrying it home.

The man's wife also looks forward to this feature of the day with a pleasantly-anxious interest; for having to act as the chancellor of the family exchequer, her being able to give effect to the household budget she has proposed to herself for the ensuing week will depend in a great measure upon the revenue returns of the Saturday—upon "father" having had a good or bad week. If he makes full time, or, better still, has had a little over-time, the proposed budget will not only be carried out in every particular, but an "available surplus" will be left, to be added to the consolidated fund which is set apart as a provision for that figurative rainy day which sickness, accident, or a temporary depression of the trade in which he is engaged may at any moment bring upon the working man. But should he, from a break-down of machinery, "sleeping-in" in the morning, or some of the other various causes that lead to working men losing time, have—in a pecuniary sense—a bad week, the household budget has to be modified; some broken, or nearly worn-out, article of furniture that was to have been replaced is "made to do" a little longer; or the purchase of the new dress-piece, which has already been deferred from week to week for a month past, is once more delayed, to see what kind of a pay another week may bring forth.

Nor is the interest in pay-day confined to the heads of the family: the children, from their own point of view, look forward to the day with as

keenly personal an interest as their parents; for
they have learned, by joyous experience, that it is
on that day that new Sunday jackets and frocks
are forthcoming, and father's "big brothers," and
lodgers, or "mates," who may be calling upon them,
are liberal in the bestowal of odd coppers upon "the
young uns," and toffy, cake, and toys, as a natural
consequence, abound. And while the fact that Saturday is the pay-day of the working classes proper
—the skilled and unskilled workmen who labour for
others at a stipulated rate of wages—makes the day
an important and interesting one to those classes, it
renders it of equally great, or perhaps still greater,
importance to that very numerous class of retail
tradesmen who depend exclusively upon the custom
of the working classes, and who do a large proportion
of their business on Saturdays.

However small or precarious may be the income
of working men individually, the aggregate income
of the working classes is a very large one, and at
the same time a very rapidly and continuously circulating one, the bulk of which has necessarily to
be expended as soon as obtained; and these facts,
taken in conjunction with the circumstances of the

income being a weekly one, and paid on a Saturday, gives a special tone, both in extent and character, to Saturday trading in working-class localities. We are told that

> " Man wants but little here below,
> Nor wants that little long."

But with respect to the working man, it would be more accurate, if less poetical, to say, " Man *gets* but little here below;" and, looking at the present state of commercial morality, and the laws bearing upon adulteration, it may be added, "Nor gets that little good." But though the individuál portion of the working man may be small, many littles, we know, make a mickle; and the task of supplying the great body of the working classes with food and clothing, and such other of the more or less essential appurtenances of civilised life as they are in a position to command, is one of muckle might; and as the working-class housekeeper lays-in the bulk of her week's provisions on Saturday, much of this great work has to be concentrated into that day. The "note of preparation" for the Saturday trading begins to be heard towards noon on Friday. On the latter day butchers kill and cut-up; grocers "make-up" innu-

merable pounds, half-pounds, and quarters of pounds
(which, if subsequently weighed in the balance, are
but too frequently found wanting) of the articles on
which there will be a run next day; and provision-
dealers, greengrocers, and other tradesmen engaged
in the victualling department, lay-in and sort the
extra stock necessary to meet the demands of the
coming day. And when the shops close, the preparations for the morrow still go on through the
watches of the night; for throughout the night, and
the small hours of the morning, the wagons of the
market-gardeners, and the trains bringing farm-
produce and all kinds of " perishable" provisions,
continue to pour immense quantities of stores into
central dépôts, whence they are again rapidly distributed among the retail tradesmen with whom the
working classes deal. For some time after opening
shop on Saturday morning, the shop- and stall-keep-
ers and their army—always greatly enlarged for the
Saturday's campaign—of assistants are busily engaged in arranging their goods so that they may
show to advantage, and be at the same time easily
get-at-able. The disposition of the goods completed,
the banners of trade-war are unfurled in the shape

of bills and boards, bearing some strange (trade) de-
vice, and inscriptions intimating that "competition
is defied" by, or that "small profits and quick returns" is the motto of, the houses trading under
the various standards which are raised aloft or borne
about by those useful, if unpicturesque, modern stan-
dard-bearers, the sandwich-men.

There is comparatively little shopping or marketing done before dinner—firstly, because, Saturday
being cleaning-up day, the thriftier housekeepers
make a rule of getting through their house-work
before "tidying themselves up" to go to market;
and secondly, because, even if their household arrangements would admit of their going out in the
morning, many of them have not the pecuniary
wherewith for marketing until the week's wages are
brought home. During the afternoon the groceries,
and such other articles as, being sold at fixed prices,
allow little room for bargain-making, are laid in; but
it is not till towards six or seven o'clock in the evening that the marketing proper sets in with full force,
and then a change comes o'er the spirit of the scene.
The gas of the provision, greengrocery, and other
establishments having out-door stands, is turned on

with a prodigality that recks not of prognostications of an impending exhaustion of our coal-fields; and the "supers," who do the walk-up part of the Saturday-night business, dance about their stands energetically soliciting custom, and continuously, and with all the force and determination that comes of trade rivalry, roar out their trade-cries of "Buy, buy, buy! Come on, ladies; great bargains here to-night, look you; take them away at your own prices this time. Here's your sort; none of your cagmag at this establishment, understand." The main streets and markets are filled to a "scrouging" extent by the marketing parties, who are easily distinguishable by their large market-baskets, which are mostly carried by the women, though some of them are attended by their husbands, who act as basket-bearers and light porters generally, but are sternly precluded from taking any part in the actual marketing, the female mind alone being capable of successfully competing with and "beating-down" the practised and mendacious retailer who deals in those descriptions of provisions the prices of which are constantly fluctuating more or less, and in buying which there is consequently scope for a little judicious cheapening.

The itinerant dealers in boot-laces, matches, pins, and other unconsidered trifles in the small and hardware lines, range themselves along the edge of the pavement, and set up their several cries; street-bands and minstrels take up their stand at favourite corners, and contribute their very considerable quota to the general din; and the whole scene becomes one of the utmost activity and bustle, and makes, upon the whole, one of the most animated and characteristic phases of working-class life in this country, and illustrates perhaps more strikingly than any other phase of their social life, the magnitude, importance, and collective wealth of the working classes.

The first object of the Saturday marketing is the purchase of the joint, or the roasting or boiling piece for the Sunday dinner, and Mrs. Jones's first proceeding, on going out to market, is to take a critical survey of the butchers' shops. Presently pausing in front of one of them, a salesman of the establishment springs to her side, and glibly uttering his war-cry, "Buy, buy, buy! beef, pork, mutton; buy, buy!" commences rapidly sharpening his knife, as though he intended to cut her up upon the spot. "What can we do for you, mum?" he goes on, calming down a little, and ceasing the knife-sharpening, but still speaking with professional rapidity and jerkiness; "nice little piece here, just suit you; prime beef, five and three-quarters, and scarcely an ounce of bone in it; can have it for three-and-six, that's under eightpence a-pound!"

"Well, I don't think you've anything that'll suit me to-day," says Mrs. Jones, beginning to move away.

"O, don't go away yet, mum," says the butcher hastily, and laying a slightly-restraining grasp upon her; "I'm sure we can accommodate you. Just look here, now; here's a nice profitable boiling piece you can have cheap."

"What do you want for that?" asks Mrs. Jones, ignoring the boiling piece, and pointing to a nice little leg of mutton on which she has had her eye from the first, and fully means purchasing if she can make a satisfactory bargain with the butcher.

"That, mum?" says the butcher; "that—that's a bit of very prime mutton, that is; as good a bit as ever you had a knife in, I'll go bail, and chance where the next came from. It ought to be nine-and-a-half, but, as I want to make a regular customer of you, we'll say nine for this time."

"I can't afford that," says Mrs. Jones, shaking her head.

"But just look at it," says the butcher, taking up the mutton; "just feel it yourself, and I know you'll say it's as fine a bit of meat as ever you laid a finger on."

"O, it's a good-enough bit of meat; I ain't denying that," says Mrs. Jones; "but nine is too much for me;" and again she begins to move away.

"Well, now, come, what *will* you give?" asks the butcher with an air of great candour.

"Well, if you like to take eight," answers Mrs. Jones, "I'll have it."

"O, I couldn't do that," says the butcher; "it stood *me* in that, it did really; but I tell you what I'll do: you shall have it at eight-and-a-half, and that's giving you a bargain."

"You'll give a bit of suet in, won't you?" says Mrs. Jones questioningly.

"Very well, then," says the butcher resignedly; "we won't spoil a bargain for sake of a bit of suet."

And so the leg is weighed and paid for, and Mrs. Jones goes on her marketing way satisfied; and if she has only got just weight she *has* made a reason-

ably good purchase, as eightpence - halfpenny per
pound can scarcely be considered dear for good leg
of mutton at a time when, either from a real scarcity
or the operations of the dealers, butcher's meat is at
cattle-plague prices.

Mrs. Jones's next visit will be to the butterman's,
where, after smelling, tasting, and otherwise testing a
large variety of samples, she decides upon the quality
and quantity of the goods she will take ; and, having
"beaten down" the shopkeeper a halfpenny in the
pound on the butter, or failing that, prevailed upon
him to " take something off" the sum-total of the
purchase-money for the cheese, butter, and bacon,
she proceeds to the market, where, for about an hour,
she will be actively engaged in a series of cheapening encounters with greengrocers and general dealers,
and in the majority of instances she will be successful in her economic endeavours, for the dealers look
upon the cheapening process as so much a thing of
course that they almost invariably allow for it in
naming their first price ; the art of cheapening,
upon the part of the intending purchaser, who also
regards the dealer's first-named price as a merely
proximate one, being to hit the exact "sticking-

place." Like most other things, the practice of cheapening, or "beating down," is useful in its place; but it is occasionally carried to a reprehensible extent, as a very characteristic "case in point," which came under my notice a few weeks since, will serve to show. A lady came up to a stall on which there was a small "remainder" of apples, of which the dealer was anxious to dispose, as he wanted to go home "cleared out."

"What will you take for these?" asked the bargain-hunter, beginning to examine the apples.

"Well, as I want to go home," answered the stall-keeper, "you can have the lot for fivepence."

"I'll give you sevenpence," said the lady, who had evidently understood him to say eightpence.

"He said fivepence," put in her husband, who was standing by as basket-bearer.

"*Did* you say fivepence?" she asked.

"Yes, that was the price, m'm," said the dealer, smiling.

"*Well, then, I'll give you fourpence,*" she said, as coolly as possible.

"Take them away," answered the dealer curtly, at the same time regarding his customer with a look of very justifiable disgust, for hers was the cheapening not of the thrifty housekeeper, but of the inveterate screw.

By nine o'clock, although the streets and markets are still crowded, and the marketing, with all its attendant bustle, going briskly on, the huge piles of provisions in shops and markets have perceptively diminished, and the earlier market parties, with their baskets filled to their utmost capacity, begin to wend their way homewards. On reaching home Mrs. Jones turns out and examines her various purchases, and takes stock of the general result of her marketing, and, on counting up the total cost, unwittingly bears testimony to the fact that gold *has* materially depreciated in value, by observing that money doesn't go so far now as it used to do, however careful you are. Although Saturday marketing is preëminently woman's work, there are a number of misguided male beings—unmarried men, who " find themselves," and put not their trust in landladies; and married men of the skinflint and mollicoting persuasions, who foolishly imagine that they are better hands at a bargain than their better-halves — who insist upon doing their own marketing; but these miserable intruders upon "the wife's dominion" are, as might naturally be expected, extensively "done" by the dealers; and I can only say with the ladies, serve 'em right too.

Saturday marketing, involving as it does "scrouging" through crowded streets, chaffering with shopkeepers and marketmen, and carrying about for an hour or two a large, and on the return journey heavily-loaded, basket, is by no means light work; but still, to the working-class housekeeper it is a labour of love, and is always thankfully performed; for it is a bad time for the working man's family when, from the bread-winner being sick or unable to obtain employment, the mother has not wherewith to go to market on Saturday.

VERY CHEAP LITERATURE.

THE present is preëminently and avowedly the age of cheap literature. Cheap daily newspapers, equal in every respect to " our high-priced contemporaries," are numerous, and cheap weekly ones are ditto, though it cannot be said of the latter class of papers that they are, as a rule, anything like equal in point of literary excellence to their high-priced contemporaries. The cheap periodicals in extensive circulation are too numerous and of too diversified a character to be mentioned here. Railway, Parlour, Shilling, Useful, and other cheap "Libraries" have brought a great variety of books within the reach of readers of very humble means, and the books necessary for a complete course of self-education can be obtained for a few shillings. "Shakespeare's Complete Works" are advertised for sale for one shilling; and a really handsome, useful, and well-edited copy of these matchless works may be had for three shillings and sixpence; while "People's" and "Popular" editions have placed the works of the great authors of modern times within the reach of all who are capable of appreciating their beauties. Nor is the cheapness of cheap literature limited to the price at which it is in the first instance published. From the prices marked on their cheap garments, Messrs. Moses and Son, Samuel Brothers, and other cheap tailors, inform their customers and the public generally there is "no abatement." But it is not so with books. From the prices marked on those articles a very considerable abatement may be obtained by the economically-inclined purchaser, as there are many bookselling firms that publicly announce that twopence in the shilling is allowed on all books purchased from their establishments; and to those who do not object to having their books with a little of the gloss of newness worn off them, the "surplus lists" of Mudie's and other circulating libraries, and the establishments of the great second-hand booksellers, offer a still cheaper means of obtaining books.

But in the cheapest depth of cheap literature

there is a cheaper depth still, and this lowest depth of cheapness is the one attained by the street booksellers. By the street bookseller I do not mean the man who keeps a second-hand bookshop, has a stall in the street in front of his shop, and prices ticketed upon his books, but the itinerant bookseller who takes up his stand in markets and squares, and at street-corners, taking his stock about with him in a hand-barrow, and disposing of it by Dutch auction. These men are generally to be found in all large towns, but they abound chiefly in the metropolis—in the poorer and more densely-populated localities of which they ply their trade with the greatest success. A few of this class of tradesmen deal in new books, their stock consisting of the remainders of works that have failed to "take" with the reading public, and "made-up" works manufactured expressly for this trade; but the majority of them—the representative men of the profession—deal exclusively in old books. How these men obtain the books which they offer for sale I know not, that being a mystery sacred to "the trade." Probably they are an amalgamation of "odd lots," "small parcels," and the last lots of the "clearance

sale" of the stock of some defunct lending-library
or book-club, or "the effects" of some legitimate
second-hand bookseller; but, how ever or where ever
obtained, their stock-in-trade is both extensive and
various.   They have works of all sizes, from twenty-
five volume editions to eight-paged pamphlets; and
of all kinds, from church-services, books of sermons,
and technical works upon the arts and sciences, to
lives of highwaymen, comic reciters, and Fistiana.
Though old, their books are generally in good condition, and to the philosophic or speculative mind
they would doubtless offer much "food for reflection."   The books which come into the hands of
the street bookseller, it may be taken for granted,
have "in their time played many parts," for no book
would be brought to this last stage of book life—this
last city of refuge between them and the scales of
the waste-paper merchant, or the counter of the
provision-dealer—at one fell swoop.   They have, it
is evident upon the face—or rather the binding—of
the subject, "seen better days;" and were they but
endowed with speech, many of them could doubtless
unfold tales of their own vicissitudes as interesting
as any recorded in their printed pages.   On almost

every volume which the street bookseller "offers to your notice," a "life history" might be founded.

Through what scenes may not the neatly-bound volume of namby-pamby poems published forty years ago, on the fly-leaf of which is written, in an elegant lady's hand, "To Miss Rose Harding, from her ever-loving friend, the authoress," have passed ere it found its way into the hands of the man who has just "knocked it down" for twopence? Here is a large old-fashioned prayer-book, on the fly-leaf of which is written, "This book is affectionately presented to James Gordon, on the occasion of his leaving home, by his loving mother." Poor loving mother! let us hope that her son came to a nobler end than the book she presented to him when he went away to fight his own battle with the world. Next to the prayer-book is an old *Robinson Crusoe*, in which is written, in a round schoolboy hand, the following terrible warning, which, though ostensibly addressed to an "honest friend," is clearly meant to apply to readers of predatory proclivities:

> " Steal not this book, my honest friend,
> For fear the gallows be your end ;
> And when you die the Lord will say,
> ' Where is that book you stole away ?'

And if you say you cannot tell,
The Lord will send you down to hell."

On the blank-leaf of the well-preserved copy of the *Annual Register* for 1792, which I have just purchased, at what I agree with the bookseller in considering "the very low price" of fourpence, is engraved the name and coat-of-arms of a baronet, and yet it has come to the pass of being sold in the street for fourpence; and other portions of the bookseller's stock may, for aught I know to the contrary, have had a still greater fall. But from whatever height they may have fallen, or through whatever scenes of more prosperous and respectable book life they may have passed to their present low estate, here they are now, gathered together in the hand-barrow of the street bookseller, ready to be " offered up" and " knocked down" to the patrons of very cheap literature.

The street bookseller must be a man of some education, he must be well up in the technicalities of the publishing and bookselling trades, and above all he must be proficient in the George-Robins style of eloquence, else will he not succeed in his business; for cheap as are his wares, they must be energetically

" cracked up," or they will " hang" upon his hands.
These booksellers have a peculiar method of classi-
fying the works which they offer for sale, and are
adepts in altering or adding to the title of their books
in a telling manner. All works having the remotest
bearing upon law, medicine, gardening, or other professional subjects, are described under the general
heading of " Every man his own lawyer," doctor,
&c. Works touching how ever slightly upon mari-
time affairs are invariably described as chronicles of
the lives and adventures of pirates and sea-robbers ;
and works relating in any way to crime or the crimi-
nal classes are offered for sale as the lives of highwaymen. Readers of all tastes, and especially those of
theological tastes, will find something to suit them
in the stock of the street bookseller. In his stock
old controversial works, and books of sermons, are extremely plentiful, and are sold under the general
heading of " Complete Family Devotions," at from a
penny to threepence per volume; while hymn and
prayer-books, which are equally abundant, are sold at
a penny or twopence each. After religious works,
works of fiction—generally old three-volume editions
of forgotten novels, though copies of the *Waverleys,*

Gil Blas, Don Quixote, and other old standard works are occasionally to be met with—are the most numerous, and are sold at prices ranging from threepence to a shilling each. Books of voyages and travels afford the widest scope for the peculiar eloquence of the bookseller, and this class of books sell remarkably well, bringing from fourpence to half-a-crown each, according to their size; voyages round the world commanding the best prices. Historical works, and especially Histories of England (which are invariably described as embracing a period extending from the Roman invasion up to twelve o'clock last night), sell well, bringing from twopence to ninepence a volume; and odd volumes of the *Spectator*, and the cabinet editions of Knight's and Lardner's works, bring about the same prices; while volumes of the old *Penny* and *Saturday Magazines* sell at from ninepence to a shilling each. Scientific and mechanical works command very little sale, and are consequently very cheap; comparatively modern works in good condition, and originally published at twelve and fifteen shillings per volume, selling for fourpence and sixpence a volume. Poetry brings very poor prices, and in disposing of this class of goods, which one would suppose might afford great opportunity for the exercise of the florid eloquence of an auctioneer, the booksellers singularly enough display little of their usual oratory, except in the case of one old Irishman who has been many years in the trade, who will dwell long and lovingly upon the merits of " *swate* Tommy Moore" whenever he has any of the works of the great Irish bard to sell. I have myself bought a large edition of Wordsworth's *Excursion* from one of these street booksellers for twopence. I have seen *Lallah Rookh* knocked down at three-pence, and a complete edition of Burns's works sold for sixpence ; while the poetical works of less-known or anonymous writers are generally "got rid of" by being " thrown in" with some "lot" for which the auctioneer finds it difficult to get a pur-chaser.

The street bookseller takes up his stand in the square or street in which he is going to carry on his business for the evening between six and seven o'clock. His first proceeding is to uncover and ar-range his goods, and his next (in the winter months) to light and fix in its place the naphtha lamp which he carries with him. While he has been thus engaged in getting his migratory establishment in order, a small knot of loungers and intending purchasers have gathered around him, and he then steps on to the small box or stool which serves him for a platform, and commences to address this group of listeners, with the twofold purpose of explaining his business and attracting a larger audience. "Gentlemen," he will commence, "I have brought you down a nice little lot of goods this evening—goods of a class that you will rarely have an opportunity of meeting with; and as I do not wish to take any of them back with me, if you will only buy quick, I will sell cheap." He will then dilate upon the special merits of the various classes of works he is going to offer for sale until a good audience has assembled around him, and he then proceeds to business. "The first work which I shall offer to your notice this evening, gentlemen," he says, taking up a set of books tied together by a piece of twine, "is a novel in three volumes, entitled *The Monastery, or the One-Handed Monk,* by Sir Walter Scott. Now, gentlemen, this is a work of startling interest, that will make your hair stand on end, like the quills upon the *frightful* porcupine. There is no mistake about this work: it is by the great Sir Walter Scott, better known as the Wizard of the North; and understand me, gentlemen, it is not only a work of the most thrilling interest and tenderest pathos, but it is also a particularly appropriate work to be read at the present day, since it contains a full and authentic account of the modes of life practised in monasteries, convents, nunneries, and similar institutions, and should therefore be read by every person who takes an interest in or wishes to be enlightened upon the great convent question which is at present agitating the country. This work," the eloquent auctioneer continues, "was originally published at thirty-one and sixpence, but if I was to stand here from now till this time next week *I* should not get that sum for it; but because I offer it for less do not suppose that the work is any the less in value. I shall not ask you thirty-one-and-six for it, nor yet even half of that sum. No; for this well-bound and well-preserved three-volume copy of the *Monastery* I can take at a word three shillings. Will no one give three shillings for this capital work?" resumes the bookseller, after a brief pause. " Well, if you won't come to my price, I'll endeavour to come to yours. I won't say two-and-nine—two-and-six—two-and-three. I won't dwell at two-and-a-penny; the first that hands me up the money shall be the buyer. Here, two shillings for it." Here another pause ensues; but no one handing up the money, this "Cheap Jack" among books continues his discourse.

"Really, gentlemen," he observes in an injured tone, "one would think, for a moment, you were either short of money or wanted judgment. Not give two shillings for a first-class work like this! Well, if you've got no money, I'll make you wish you had some. I won't say one-and-nine for the novel of startling interest; here, take it away at one-and-six. I won't ask one-and-three; it's a scandalous price, but—as times are hard and money scarce, I can't avoid it—a shilling for it, and if you can match it at any house in the trade for three times the amount, I'll give it you for nothing." Here there is a very long pause, but still there is no sign of a purchaser; and the salesman then observes in a still more deeply-injured tone, "O, well, gentlemen, if I can't get a shilling for the class of goods that I am now offering to you, why, down they go in a moment, and if I once lay them down I won't offer them for the same price again to-night;" and he stoops as if to lay the books down, but suddenly straightening himself again, and looking as though he had resolved to do something of a desperate nature, he exclaims: "Well, just look here! If it's as hard to draw money out of your pockets as it is to take a wheelbarrow through the eye of a needle, or for an elephant to dance upon a butterfly's back, I'll do it. I'll make you buy! I won't ask a shilling for the three-volume work; it's a thing I've never done before, but to show you that I'm not confined to a price I won't even say tenpence for it; nine-and-a-half; here, take it away at nine, and I won't take the tenth part of a farthing less, sell it or never sell it, buy it who may." This is final; the climax of cheapness has been reached, and after a short pause a person in the crowd, which is now a tolerably large one, exclaims, "Here you are!" and handing up nine-pence becomes the purchaser of the " first lot" of the evening. Having now established a sale, our purveyor of cheap literature is less diffuse over succeeding "lots" of the same class, getting rid of his sliding scale of reduction of price by briefly observing that as he has begun the game he won't raise the price.

And, indeed, he generally has to lower it, for it is only for such standard works of fiction as may occasionally fall into his hands that the street bookseller can get more than sixpence. When the sale for one class of works falls off, the street trader in books "shows you up a work of another kind." Novels are, perhaps, succeeded by medical works, of which the first lot offered for sale may be an old volume of the *Pharmaceutical Journal.* "This work," our bookseller will say, showing it to his audience, "is the *Pharmaceutical Journal, or every Man his own Doctor,* and contains recipes by all the most eminent physicians, surgeons, and apothecaries of the day, for the cure of all diseases. And unless they can say—which, of course, no person can—that they will never be ill, no person should be without such a work. Now, gentlemen, this work contains hundreds of recipes for the self-cure of all diseases, but if it only contained one such recipe, it would be worth far more money than I shall ask you for it. Although, like all medical works, this was originally published at a very high price, and would cost in the ordinary way of trade something like twelve or fifteen shillings, I can afford to take the very low price of half-a-crown for it." And here the sliding scale of reduction is again brought into action until the work is finally knocked down for fourpence. Other classes of books are enlarged upon in an equally imaginative manner, and are disposed of at a similarly low scale of prices. The audience of the street bookseller is a shifting one, and so by the time he has gone through and sold a few of each of the various classes of works he has to offer for sale, and comes back to the class with which he commenced, the crowd around him has become in a great measure a new one, and the sales go on with unabated vigour.

One of these men will generally sell from fifty to sixty works in the course of a night, and on Saturday nights I have often known them to dispose of from 150 to 200. Of all the many classes of street tradesmen, these booksellers are the most intelligent and best educated. Many of them have, like the books which they sell, evidently seen better days, and they are a most industrious and useful class of men. During the day-time they are engaged in collecting the old and (save to and by them) unsaleable books which form their stock-in-trade. At night they have to transport their goods to the district in which they are going to hold their sales; and after giving loose to their tongues and imaginations for three or four hours, in describing the wonders which they allege are contained in the works they are offering for sale, and obtaining customers for those works, they have to pack up and trudge to their homes, which are often miles distant, through all kinds of weather. To working men who are fond of reading or desirous of improving their education, and who have a little discriminating knowledge of books, the street booksellers afford opportunities of securing books which they could never otherwise hope to possess, and the curious in old books will often find in their stock works for which they would seek in vain elsewhere. And though the exaggerated descriptions which these men give of the nature and contents of the works which they offer for sale may sometimes induce persons whose capacity of belief is greater than their knowledge of literature, to buy volumes of prosy, unintelligible controversial theology, under the impression that they are getting something of a sensational character, or to purchase a dull novel with the idea that it is an authentic historical work, the few pence for which these works are sold are, after all, better invested than if they had been spent in " goes" of gin, or pots of " fourpenny."

Although unknown, unenrolled, and unrecognised, the street booksellers may be said to be powerful members of the Society for the Diffusion of Knowledge, since by their agency, knowledge, in the shape of books, is circulated among large numbers of the working classes to whom books rarely penetrate through the ordinary channels of book circulation.

EASTER WITH THE UNWASHED.

HOWEVER insignificant some of its members may be individually—and though, like other mundane bodies, it has its faults—there can be no doubt that, considered collectively and taken "through and through," the Great Unwashed is a highly important section of the community. It is important politically, socially, and commercially, as well as by reason of its numerical superiority. But while its greatness is chiefly manifest in the more serious relations of life, it is also of importance—as Messrs. E. T. Smith, Frederick Strange, and other "enterprising lessees," could testify—in the matter of amusements and holidays; and it is with regard to the holiday phase of their life that I now propose to speak of them.

Many of the unwashed now participate in the benefits of the Saturday half-holiday movement; others indulge more or less in the worship of Saint

Monday; and in some districts there are occasional holidays in connection with local customs. These, however, are but partial or accidental holidays, and the holidays proper of the unwashed are the three great festivals of Christmas, Easter, and Whitsuntide. Of these, Easter, viewed purely as a holiday, is the greatest. Christmas is devoted more especially to the renewing of home associations and the promotion of social intercourse; and Whitsuntide coming some weeks after the " outing" season has fairly set in, the holiday zest that comes in with the spring is by that time somewhat toned down.

At Easter, however, everything is in favour of the holiday. Coming as it does just as we are fairly emerging from the cold and damp of winter, it is practically regarded as the festival of spring—the means and occasion for giving expression to that exuberantly joyous feeling which all, either consciously or unconsciously, experience under the influence of that " gladness of nature" incidental to the springtime of the year. And it has the further material advantage that the unwashed have specially favourable opportunities of "saving up" for it. Even in their pleasures, those of the working classes who would enjoy them thoroughly must be provident; must "save up" for them—provide for their *sunny* as well as rainy days. You cannot have your cake and eat it too; and the money which the million can afford to devote to holiday-making purposes being strictly limited in amount, those of them who have previously been indulging in outings to Hampton or Kew, or day excursions to the seaside, have necessarily to "draw it mild" in the Whitsun week. But at Easter this serious drawback does not exist, as during the deadly, dull season that intervenes between it and Christmas the million are under no temptation to fritter away their pocket-money in small outings.

As soon as the unwashed have got over their Christmas festivities they begin to prepare for Easter, which, in addition to being the first out-door holiday of the year and the legitimate opening of the holiday season, is also the fashionable time (among the great unwashed) for the inauguration of new summer clothing. Jack puts by so much out of his wages, and watches for the advertisements, in which, as spring draws near, the "merchant tailors" set forth the manifold excellences of "our fifty-shilling suits."

Matilda, who is in the millinery and dressmaking line, also tries to save a trifle from her scanty earnings, and studies the fashions with a view to making such modifications in her last summer's dress as shall enable her to appear—as becomes her profession—in the latest style. The domestic Susan, who is her own minister of finance, devotes her mental energies to the task of arranging such a plan of expenditure for her next quarter's wages as will admit of her having a new summer bonnet or dress; and even the older family couples, when discussing questions of household expenses, will often observe as a reason for special economy that " Easter is coming, you know." And so, when Easter arrives all sections are generally prepared to celebrate it in a worthy manner.

As Easter is avowedly an out-door holiday—a holiday to be spent, if possible, in some green spot of earth, where you may

> " breathe the breath
> Of the cowslip and primrose sweet,
> With the sky above your head
> And the grass beneath your feet"—

those of the unwashed whose lot it is to dwell in stony, smoky, overcrowded towns and cities are natu-

rally among its most enthusiastic devotees. Take
for example the unwashed of the metropolis, whose
doings in this respect are in a great measure representative. To them there are few places that offer
greater attractions than Greenwich; and of that
portion of the pleasure-loving million who patronise
this most attractive of London suburbs on Easter
Mondays I am now going to speak. The unwashed
are wise in their generation, and, acting upon the
principle that there is a time for everything, enter
into their enjoyments with a gusto which it is a
positive pleasure to witness, and is also very catching.
Indeed, I think there could be no better test of a
man's capability of enjoyment than a day out with
the million; for if he neither experiences pleasure at
witnessing *their* pleasure, nor is himself smitten with
the prevailing spirit, he may safely come to the me-
lancholy conclusion that he is inaccessible to joyous
influences.

Early on Easter Monday morning Greenwich
begins to show tokens of the coming invasion of
pleasure-seeking. The park and Blackheath (which,
as Londoners are aware, adjoins the park) are the
chief centres of attraction, and here the stall pro-

prietors—the purveyors of eatables, drinkables, and
such sports as Aunt Sally and penny shooting-galleries—are early astir getting their itinerant establishments in order. The streets, too, are busy with
carts bearing ginger-beer, oranges, nuts, and other
more solid provisions, to the scene of action; and up
Blackheath-hill may be seen streaming the gipsy-
like donkey-men of the heath, with their studs of
donkeys and broken-down hacks and cab-horses increased twentyfold to meet the demands of this day.
On foot and by the early trains begin to arrive
parties of street "niggers," numbers of those "efficient quadrille bands," consisting of harp, cornet,
and violin, who play at "hops" during the winter
season, and go " on the busk" to watering-places and
other fashionable resorts in the summer; and troops
of the ragged, importunate toy merchants, who
sell "jolly noses," dolls, paper wreaths, and the other
grotesque sundries with which it is the wont of many
young Cockneys to adorn themselves when "outing"
on such occasions as Easter Monday or the Derby-
day. About noon the pleasure-seekers begin to
pour into the town by rail and river, and from that
hour till about three in the afternoon there is a con-

tinuous stream of visitors passing from pier and
station into the park, and through the park on to the
heath.

On entering the park it becomes evident that

" On with the dance, let joy be unconfined,"

is the animating principle of action among the assembled thousands of smiling, happy-looking holiday-
makers. " The efficient quadrille bands," concertina-
players, and even organ-grinders, are fully employed
in discoursing dance-music to large parties, whose
dancing, if not particularly graceful, is at any rate
energetic and joyous, and contrasts favourably with
the funeral-like manner in which dances are "walked
through" in fashionable society. A considerable proportion of the male performers on the light fantastic
toe are soldiers, mostly smart young fellows, who
have walked up from Woolwich, and who, belonging to gorgeously-uniformed regiments, "go down"
with the girls much better than the more quietly-
attired civilians. But there is happily such an abundance of pretty animated partners to be had, that
this circumstance does not come home very crush-
ingly to those who are for the nonce inferior, because
non-military, beings. In connection with the pro-

ceedings of the dancing section of the holiday-makers, it is satisfactory to notice that they are very liberal in "paying the piper." At the end of each dance each male dancer gives the band a penny, and as from thirty to forty couples generally stand up to each dance, the "musicians" make a pretty good thing out of an Easter Monday holiday.

The "niggers" are also doing well, and are reaping, if not a golden, at any rate a very satisfactory coppery harvest from among the crowd who are listening to them, and who, being in good humour with themselves and everybody else, are laughing heartily at the stale jokes uttered by the "banjo" or "bones" of the wandering troupe. After dancing, kiss-in-the-ring is the game most in vogue with those in the park, and especially with the courting couples, who in it find a means of combining love and amusement. Skipping-rope is another favourite sport, the rope being supplied and turned by men, who in this way earn a little money, and who appear to make a living by such means as this, brushing clothes at race-meetings, and acting generally as a sort of camp-followers to out-door holiday parties. Another game —if game it can be called—out of which many of the million manage to extract a good deal of fun, is the one traditionally incidental to Greenwich Park of running down One-Tree Hill. But as this game involves a rather free display of leg it is advisable for only such ladies as have confidence in their neatness of limb to engage in it, as otherwise they may chance to hear such disparaging criticisms as "spindle-shanky" or "gateposty" applied to their ankles.

Passing through the park-gates on, to Blackheath, you come at once upon the more decided "fun-of-the-fair" kind of amusements. The drums and trumpets, the hoarse shouts of the showmen, and the crack of the rifles at the shooting-galleries are the first sounds that greet your ears; while hobby-horses (some of them, as becomes the age of steam, worked with an engine), Aunt Sallys, penny-ice stalls, weighing-machines, and the thousand and one other accompaniments of a modern fair, meet your gaze. Into all these amusements provided for them the crowd on the heath enter heartily.

Men and women mingle with the children in patronising the hobby-horses. The show containing the heaviest woman in the world is being filled and emptied every five minutes—the statement of those

who are coming out to the effect that " she ain't half
so big as she looks on the picture," having no deter-
ring effect upon the eager sightseers, who are push-
ing in. The sea-lion, as the showman by virtue of
the poetical license of his profession styles a seal, is
also drawing good houses, as are likewise some street
tumblers, who have managed to get hold of a very
primitive, shaky-looking tent, wherein to display their
feats. Aunt Sally is being played with quite a ducal
energy ; and, at the "knock-'em-downs," the circumstance of the cocoa-nuts always dropping "in the
hole, sir," in no way damps the enthusiasm of the
players. The rifle-galleries, the weight-registering
machines, and the other too-numerous-to-be-men-
tioned holiday institutions, are also well patronised ;
nor are the refreshment-stalls neglected.

The great feature on the heath, however, is the
riding. A shilling ride round the heath is the " cor-
rect thing," and whole troops of John Gilpins are
galloping about on the Rosinantes provided for them
by the " caterers" in that line. The flying coat-
tails, the trousers rumpled up to the knee, the shaky
seat, ungainly appearance, and evident nervousness
of these riders, and their inability to control their

steeds, afford much amusement to the spectators. And much good-humoured pleasantry goes on among, and at the expense of, the girls, many of whom are induced to take rides on the donkeys. After a little coaxing from their lovers, and many fervent assurances of the docility of the animals from the proprietors, they allow themselves to be hoisted on to the donkeys' backs. Some of them discover a natural equestrian talent, and dash off screaming and laughing, and calling upon the attendants to make the animals go; while the attempts to remonstrate against the severity of the pace, or the cries to stop, of those whose doubts as to their being able to ride are realised, are rendered absurd and unintelligible by the jolting of the donkeys. Sometimes a rider of this latter class will, upon approaching a soft spot, adroitly slip off over the donkey's tail, a proceeding which has a really comic effect, and is always received with roars of laughter. A donkey-race has a decided tendency to disarrange female costume; and as the girls come in groups down " the straight run in," their streaming hair and flushed faces present a very pretty picture, to which their merry laughter is a fitting accompaniment. In the midst of all these amusements it is pleasant to notice the entire absence of drunkenness. Among the many thousands in the park and on the heath you will rarely see a single case of intoxication. No intoxicating drinks are allowed to be sold in the park; and though some enterprising beer merchants bring casks of ale on the heath, they happily, in a great measure, spoil their own sale. Their stuff—"metropolitan purge," as it is aptly styled—is usually so very bad that none returns to their tap a second time.

In such amusements as I have spoken of the great unwashed pass their great out-door holiday very merrily till the shades of evening close in, and then they begin to make their way towards the station, singing the choruses of popular songs as they go along, thus bringing the day to a harmonious conclusion.

OUT OF COLLAR.

CONSIDERING the limited and commonplace sphere of action to which they are confined, there are few who experience more frequent and abrupt changes of fortune, more ups and downs in the world, than the working classes—the utility people of the great drama of life. The position of a working man is at all times an exceedingly precarious one, and is more readily and seriously influenced by circumstances beyond his own control than the position of almost any other class of men. And, in a general way, there is nothing that so materially and frequently affects the well-being and social position of a working man, as the circumstances arising from his being out of work.

The uncertainties of our proverbially variable climate, though weighing upon all classes of society,

bear with special heaviness upon working men, affecting as they do not merely their constitutions,
but what is to many of them of even greater importance—their opportunities of working. A London fog will sometimes stop hundreds of men from
following their usual employment; and often, after
hanging about till they are wet through in the hope
that the weather may "take up," navvies and other
out-door workmen will on a rainy day have to "knock
off," wet and disheartened.

> " We're all froze out and knocking about,
> And we've got no work to do,"

sing bodies of men as they march slowly through the
streets in hard winters. Many of these bands are of
course professional mendicants, who, with an energy
and versatility worthy of a better cause, seize upon
passing events and pass themselves off as the specially unemployed of the hour. During a cotton-
famine they assume the character of factory operatives, and intimate to the public, by means of a lugu-
brious chant, that they have

> " Come all the way from Manchester,
> And have got no work to do-o-o."

Are the ribbon or silk-weaving trades slack, they do

the "pious-weaver" business, informing you in effect that

> " Providence will your charity bless,
> If you'll purchase a small religious tract
> From a pious weaver in distress."

They frequently appear as the survivors from ship-wrecks and colliery explosions; and in the same way it is their custom, when there is a sufficiently severe frost to give colour to their representation, to come out in the character of frozen-out gardeners, bricklayers, labourers, and so forth. But while the frozen-out bands who parade the streets are in the majority of instances impostors, no person having the slightest knowledge of the working classes needs to be told that at such seasons there are large numbers of working men in a state of compulsory idleness and consequent distress; and that at all seasons working men of every class are from force of uncontrollable circumstances liable to be metaphorically "frozen out" from bread-winning pursuits—to be, in their own phrase, "out of collar," that is, to be unable to obtain work when they are able to do it, and anxious to get it to do.

I have heard and read a great deal to the effect

that a man with an ordinary share of intelligence and a willing pair of hands need never want for work—that he who has health and strength may despise wealth and laugh at the frowns of Fortune— and those who cannot find employment nowadays must be idlers or dolts. The "healthy tone" of these generalisations is undeniable, and there is doubtless a certain qualified degree of truth in them. But though they may serve admirably as "tags" to "moral discourses" or speeches at a distribution of prizes to workmen, or the opening of a working-man's club, they are much too Alderman Cutish and absolute in their doctrine to be received as general or incontrovertible axioms. An ordinary share of intellect, a strong and willing pair of hands, and perseverance and industry, are all very excellent things which will stand their possessor in good stead, and enable him to pull through where less-bountifully-endowed individuals would despondingly or despairingly stick fast. But all this being admitted, practical men who have their living to get and their way to make in the world by the labour of their brains or hands know that, despite all that messieurs the utterers of muscular moralities may say,

" 'Tis not in mortals to command success."

Most mortals may, and if they are to be believed do, deserve it, but comparatively few obtain it, and some of these few secure it by means of which the preachers of the invariably success-commanding properties of perseverance, energy, and so forth could not with any conscience approve. I do not speak thus by way of complaint, but simply in order that those worthy persons who morally pat working men upon the back, and tell them that they have only to be steady and industrious, to have a willing heart and a ready hand, to be certain of rising in the world, may not suppose that I wish to imply any want of perseverance or will to work upon the part of the working classes generally, when I say that there are very few men who do not occasionally suffer from want of employment.

Spells of dull trade, like accidents, will happen ; and new inventions or discoveries, or even a change of fashion, will occasionally revolutionise a trade, or, so far as the prospects of the immediate workers in it are concerned, destroy it ; and from such causes as these it frequently happens that considerable bodies of men are thrown out of work.

Being " out of collar" is at the best a sad trial, involving, as it does, immediate loss of income, and consequent falling behind with the world. In its least aggravated form it means distress of mind, curtailment of the ordinary comforts and necessities of life, the expenditure of the little savings that may have been laid by for sickness or old age, the getting into debt in the books of the small shopkeeper; ultimately, perhaps, the breaking-up of a home, the selling of " the few sticks of furniture," and the " trapesing" across the country of the wife and family to join the bread-winner in the far-away town in which he may have again found employment. To many it means an empty cupboard, a fireless grate, scanty clothing, a starving wife and family, sickness of body and mind, brought on by these ills at a time when they are least prepared to battle with it. To some it means days of dull, weary, footsore tramping from town to town; and to all the heart-sickening uncertainty as to how long such a miserable state of things may last. A man may be fortunate, and " drop in" in a few days; but on the other hand he may be out of work for weeks, and even months; and though, by means of previous savings, credit with tradesmen to whom he is known, or assistance or monetary accommodation from friends, he may be able to procure the necessaries of life through this unproductive period, he constantly sees before him the ever-increasing rock ahead of debt. And this rock clings to and weighs him down long after he gets into employment again, for the paying-off of old scores is a work of time; and the frequency with which they are out of work makes the average of the actual earnings of many working men disagreeably small, as compared with the wages at which they are rated when they are in employment.

This is a phase of the position of a working man generally overlooked by those outside his own class. The house of a mechanic is seen poorly furnished, and himself and family scantily clad, and it is immediately said, "Here there must be waste and extravagance, for this man earns eight-and-twenty or five-and-thirty shillings"—more or less, as the case may be—" per week." And in some cases the squalor which is but too frequently found in the households of even the higher-paid portions of the working classes is undoubtedly attributable to improvidence and mismanagement; but in the majority of instances it is owing to the fact that the head of the house is often out of work for many weeks in the year, and that his real is considerably below his nominal income.

In discussing any question relative to the social position or prospects of the working classes, the "out of collar" phase of their life, and the impoverishing consequences resulting from it, should be taken into consideration. It should be remembered that it takes the working man who has a family dependent upon him months, sometimes years, to get over the disastrous effects of "a spell out of collar."

Working men, as a body, may sometimes be given to grumbling without much cause; but they are by no means wont to make loud or open complaint of the *inevitable* distresses incidental to their position in life. Even when out of work, they try to put a good face upon the matter. But while they bravely bear, they know and keenly fear and feel, the ills resulting from being "out of collar." In a large workshop, when hands are being "sacked," the wistful glances that attend the office-boy as he goes round with the notices of discharge; the anxious inquiries as to who has, or who has not, got "the bullet," as the formal note intimating that, "owing to a reduction of our establishment your services will no longer be required," is called among working men; the relieved looks of those who have not got it, and the pale faces and shaking hands which belie the affected don't-careishness of some of those who have;—all testify to the working man's dread of the grim consequences of being out of employment.

The loss of work does not, of course, affect all men in the same manner or degree. To a young unmarried man who has a few pounds and a suit or two of good clothes by him, and who is a member of a trade club, it may be a matter of comparatively little moment; while to the married man who has a wife and a number of children, who "can neither work nor want," dependent upon him, it may be a matter of life or death. The proceedings of those who are out of work are in a great measure guided by, and dependent upon, family circumstances.

In the metropolitan districts and the larger manufacturing towns of the provinces, where there are a number of establishments in the same branch of trade, there are workmen who, having been born in those districts, or settled in them early in life, never leave them, however trade may fluctuate. They may have friends or relations in the town able to afford them some assistance in time of need; they may— and in the factory and hardware towns usually do— have children at work. They are known in the neighbourhood in which they reside. By the aid of children's wages, a little assistance from friends, and credit with the small tradesmen to whom they are known, they manage, when out of work, to keep their household together until "things take a turn," and they get into employment again. This is about as *settled* a kind of life as the great body of working men can hope to attain. To those men, however, and more especially the unmarried men, who lack the means or inclination to "hang on" in any par- ticular district until they can get work there again, nothing remains but to go on tramp, or, as they gene- rally put it, go on the road.

TRAMPS AND TRAMPING.

A VERY prevalent notion of a tramp is that of a dirty, ragged, garotter-like fellow who lurches about the country, sometimes making a show of selling some trifling article, but oftener begging in a style that almost amounts to stealing—who occasionally turns up at police-courts as a casual pauper charged with tearing his clothes, and may at times be seen skulking under the trees in Hyde Park attired in a manner that is much more filthy and indecent than picturesque. But this is not the working man's idea of a tramp. For such as them he has no consideration, since he regards them—and, upon the whole, I think justly regards them—as pests to society—fellows who are too idle and dissolute to work, and too cowardly to commit any crime for which they might happily be sent from their country, for their country's good. A tramp, as understood among the working classes, is simply a working man "on the road" in quest of work, and travelling on foot for the all-sufficient reason that he has not the means of paying for railway or other conveyance, but having, as a rule, the wherewith to provide himself with a crust during the day and a humble place in which to lay his head at night. The professional mendicant species of tramp tells you, in one of his favourite ballads,

" In the days when I was hard up, not very long ago,
I suffered what can only the sons of misery know ;
Relations, friends, companions, they all turned up their nose,
And rated me a vagabond for want of better clothes."

But in a general way the working man when on tramp experiences no such treatment as this. Of course there are in the working classes, as in other ranks of life, men who, wrapping themselves in the mantle of personal prosperity, avoid as unclean, or at any rate unprofitable, those who are suffering from the "slings and arrows of outrageous fortune." But individuals of this selfish type are happily exceptional. The majority of working men have for a man on the road that fellow-feeling which makes us wondrous kind. Most of them either have been, or know that they may at any time have to go, on tramp, and so they adopt for their motto, "Be to a friend in distress like a brother," and receive a tramping fellow-craftsman in all cases with brotherly kindness, and in those instances where it is required, assist him, so far as their means enable them to do so, with food, shelter, money, or raiment, though in connection with the latter there is one mistaken kindness the tramp will do well *not* to accept—to wit, the gift of a pair of old boots. Most persons know from experience that walking any considerable distance in a new pair of boots is generally productive of painful consequences to the " poor feet ;" but the suffering caused by a new pair of boots is a mild case of boiled peas compared with the tortures which a pair of boots that have been worn to the set of another person's feet inflicts upon the unwise and unhappy tramp who attempts to wear them. At every step that he takes he will have painful occasion to curse every knob and furrow in each particular boot, for on *his* feet the knobs are *certain* to come in where the furrows should be, and excruciating tortures follow. The tramp who has once suffered from this infliction will, an there be any of the milk of human kindness in his composition, at all future times be ready to exclaim with heartfelt sincerity,

" Good Heaven, the *soles* of all my tribe defend
   From——old boots !"

All kinds of workmen are occasionally obliged to
" take to the road," but the class who are most frequently found on tramp are the mechanics who are
members of trade unions.   For them, the road is de-
prived of half its terrors and inconveniences.   The
donation which, when out of employment, they receive from their union, is sufficient to relieve them
from all apprehension of absolute starvation.   In almost every town they have their club-house, at which
they will perhaps meet some old mate, and at all
times find fellow-unionists and brother-craftsmen
who will receive them in good-fellowship, and furnish them with reliable information as to the state of
trade and the chances of obtaining employment in
the town.   But even under the most advantageous
circumstances, going on the road is anything but
pleasant, and is by the great body of working men
regarded as a mode of looking for work only to be
adopted as a last resource.   I remember a mate of
mine being discharged a week after he was married ;
the establishment in which he had been employed
being the only one of its kind in the town, and trade

being dull at the time, there was nothing left for him but to go on the road. He was most unwillingly making up his bundle ready for a start, when, owing to the firm receiving a large order, I was sent to tell him that he could have his job again. He was living in an upstairs room, and when I entered it was kneeling beside a box, selecting the necessary articles of clothing to take with him on his journey; but the instant I delivered my message he sprang to his feet with a whoop of triumph, and commenced the performance of an ecstatic break-down, in the midst of which a weak part of the flooring gave way, and one of his legs went through the ceiling of the room below, much to the consternation of its occupants. Nor is such extravagance, under similar circumstances, by any means rare. There are many men who would regard themselves as ingrates were they not to celebrate their being " shopped," after having been out of collar, by " a spree;" and I have often seen men, when they have drawn their first pay after having been out of work for a considerable time, throw the money on the ground, and then lie down and roll over it; at the same time triumphantly calling the attention of their shopmates to the fact that they, though so recently "hard up," were rolling in their riches.

When it becomes necessary to go on tramp, two mates generally try to go together; sometimes, if they are both young and unmarried, and especially if they have been fellow-apprentices, they will make an arrangement to the effect, either that neither will take work in a town where the other cannot get work too, or, that if one gets work before the other, he shall keep both until his companion also "drops in." These bargains are almost always kept, not only with scrupulous honour, but in the kindest possible spirit.

The summer, as might naturally be expected, is the pleasantest season for being on the road, and it is also the cheapest, as at that time of year there is always a chance of getting a "fill" of fruit or vegetables while passing through the agricultural districts that lie between large manufacturing towns. If the weather be very hot, it is a frequent practice for men on tramp to travel by night and sleep during the hottest part of the day; a plan that saves much fatigue, and to the tramp is not the inconvenience that it would be to an artist or pleasure-seeking pedestrian tourist travelling in search of the picturesque. Tramps have seldom an eye for the natural beauties of rural scenery, and a good field of turnips conveniently near to the roadside, or an orchard whose trees overhang the hedge, have far greater attractions for them than the grandest landscape that was ever described in verse or transferred to canvas. In this respect tramps are generally something like a London-bred workman who came to work in the provincial workshop in which I was an apprentice. On the Sunday after he came I took him into the country to a spot which commanded a view of beautifully varied scenery, which artists and other lovers of the beautiful came great distances to look upon, and which has more than once afforded subjects for the brushes of some of the modern masters. The day was calm and gloriously sunny, and mountain, valley, and woodland for miles around seemed literally bathed in the beauty-enhancing sunlight, while the river, whose winding course could be traced as far as the eye could reach, glistened and sparkled as though it had been liquid crystal. Altogether the scene was one which it would have been thought no man could have beheld unmoved, and when it burst on our sight, upon turning an angle of the hill from which the best view of the landscape could be obtained, I began to descant, with all the enthusiasm of youth, on the beauty of the scenery which met my admiring gaze in every direction. My companion looked around him for a minute or two in a silence which I took to be that of rapturous admiration at beholding a sight not only extremely lovely in itself, but of an entirely novel character to him, and which it would reasonably have been supposed would have appeared as a vision of bliss to a city-bred workman. I was accordingly both astonished and disgusted when he broke in upon my rhapsody by exclaiming in a contemptuous tone, *" O, blow your beautiful scenery! I wish to the Lord I could see a public-house; that would be the scenery for me."* This Cockney I found, when I came to have a greater experience of working men, was by no means an exception in holding the opinion that the beautiful and practical are one ; for since the day when I stood on the hillside with him, and was shocked by his horrible though honest practicability, I have met thousands of working men who, like him, considered a public-house the most attractive feature of a rural landscape.

But though tramps as a rule are unable to appreciate the natural beauties which often present themselves to the view of the traveller along the main roads of England, they are not without methods of relieving the monotony of pedestrian travel. Speculations as to the probabilities of their finding employment in the town at which they are next going to call, and narrations of adventures met with on previous tramps (in the telling of which a little drawing on the imagination for the sake of effect is in no way objected to), serve to shorten the road. Sometimes, if only travelling for one day, or, in order to make sure of work, or to have a Sunday in any particular town, or when they have any other special object in view, a tramp will walk forty or fifty miles in a day ; but under ordinary circumstances, twenty-five miles is considered a good average day's walk.

In tramping, as in everything else, experience maketh wise ; and the experienced tramp, when on the road, suffers less in person, purse, and wardrobe than his inexperienced brethren. The practised tramp has ingenious methods of fastening on buttons, or repairing a broken brace. He can generally do a bit of extempore tailoring, and can, at a push,

wash his own shirt and stockings; and he has got
rid of that fallacious notion, as erroneous as it is
uncleanly, that it hardens the feet to leave them unwashed, and bathes them at least once a day whenever it is possible to do so. He is great on the
subject of shoes, and knows that the best kind for
tramping in are a strong pair of lace-ups that have
never been cobbled, and which have been sufficiently
worn to bring them to the set of the feet. When
on the road, the old tramp always keeps his boots
well greased, and is generally in possession of cheap
and cunning recipes for the manufacture of dubbin,
which shall at the same time soften the leather and
render it impervious to damp. He is weather-wise,
and will read the approach of a storm in signs that
would altogether escape the notice of a young tramp.
He has a beneficial knowledge of what may be called
road-craft, and has a practical acquaintance with the
"ins and outs" of many roads. On coming to the
commencement of a long stretch of soft or grass-
bordered road, he will, in dry weather, take off his
boots, sling them across his shoulders, and walk bare-
foot : by this means saving his boots and easing and
cooling his feet; and if, from being a long time on

tramp, his feet become blistered or inflamed, he can doctor them skilfully. The old tramp, too, knows the most advantageous manner of laying out small sums of money. He will not, like the inexperienced, buy twopennyworths of bread and cheese, or expend his coppers in the purchase of the low-priced but really dear productions of small cook-shops. He adopts the more profitable plan of buying his provisions in the rough, and by weight, and as he knows the names and prices of all the "odd bits" in the butchers' shops, he can indulge in the luxury of flesh-meat much oftener than an inexperienced man, and can vary the dressing and cooking of his coarse and limited food to a surprising extent. It often happens that while waiting for an answer to an application for work, a man on the road has to remain in a town for a day or two. In this case, the tramp who "knows his way about" understands what to do. In towns that are large enough to make it worth the while of men in search of work to stop in them for any considerable time, on the chance of something "turning up," there is generally a free reading-room, or one to which admission can be gained on payment of a penny. To one of these rooms the tramp, after

he has performed his morning ablutions and made
the most of his scanty wardrobe, betakes himself, and
there he stays reading, or affecting to read, until
evening, when he goes out to meet fellow-craftsmen
from whom he hopes to get intelligence of a job.
He only goes back to his inn at an hour when those
who "use the house" are assembled, and at that time
he can usually rely upon a hearty welcome. He can
always favour the assembled guests with the adventures he has met with on the road, and as a rule
he can sing a comic song—generally an Irish one,
as, by merely rolling his trousers up to the knees,
and using the poker as a shillelagh, he can give
it in character—in a superior (public-house) style.
In a word, he is a man of the world, and "good
company," and is regarded as an acquisition by the
circle who meet to have their evening pipe and
glass in the large well-warmed kitchen of the Hand
and Hammer. For the time being he is looked
upon by the tribe of the Hand and Hammer as their
special guest—a brave of some kindred and friendly
tribe. They applaud the stories of the son of the long
bow and brother of the tough yarn, while he grate-
fully smokes the pipe of peace and drinks the glass

of friendship with them.   If he has to continue on "the path" they will assist him, if need be, with the sinews of war, while, should it so fall out that he becomes a dweller in those parts, and, when in collar, resorts to the happy drinking-ground of the Hand and Hammer, he soon becomes a brother and chief of the tribe.

If there be any romance connected with so essentially distressful a thing as being out of collar, it is the romance of the road; and tramping experiences and adventures are stock subjects of workshop conversation.   Upon the day when I entered upon my apprenticeship I was much astonished and mystified by a scrap of conversation on the subject of " the road" which I overheard.   In the dinner-hour I was standing beside a stove around which a number of workmen were grouped, when one of them observed:

" Brassy Harry came into town last night."

" Ay ?" exclaimed the others.

" Yes," said the first speaker, "he's been on the road five weeks ; and he came forty miles yesterday."

At this statement there was a general elevation of eyebrows, upon which the speaker added, in an explanatory tone, "But he got a good lift from a farmer."

Now, the phrase, "on the road," was at this time indissolubly connected in my mind with visions of dashing highwaymen mounted on powerful coal-black steeds, and I was sufficiently well read in the Waverleys to know the meaning of lifting cattle, but of the technicalities of tramping I knew nothing. The impression which this scrap of conversation left upon my mind consequently was, that Brassy Harry was some renowned modern freebooter on whom the mantles of Messrs. Dick Turpin and Rob Roy had descended, but of whom I had not hitherto had the good fortune to hear. I was therefore much surprised to discover, on the following day, that a pale, wayworn-looking man whom I saw standing at the workshop gate was Brassy Harry. I began to wonder how he dared show himself thus openly, and, above all, what he could possibly want at a workshop gate.

"Want?" said the workman to whom I applied for enlightenment. "Why, what should he want? He wants a job."

"Wants a job?" I exclaimed in astonishment.

" Yes. He's a brass-moulder ; that's why we call him Brassy ; and he's been out of collar and tramping for the last five weeks, poor chap !"

I now saw the mistake under which I had been labouring, and was very glad when I heard later in the day that Brassy had got a job, and was to start on the following morning. And on the following morning he did start, as I had especial cause to remember. On that day, while eating the " snack" which I had brought with me by way of lunch, I threw a crust of bread under the stove, and had scarcely done so when I received from Brassy a ringing box on the ear, which almost knocked *me* under the stove. Before I could ask " What's that for ?" Brassy, in a tone of voice that was kindly rather than otherwise, said to me:

" Excuse me clouting thee, my lad ; but happen it'll do thee good, for perhaps it'll teach thee never to waste a bit o' bread again. Unless thou hast better luck than most o' thy kind, the day'll come when thou'll be glad on a bit o' bread like that you've chucked away. When you're on t' road you'll think turnips good eating, and look on bread as Sunday grub."

After this little incident we became the best of friends, and many a cunning " wrinkle" did he put me up to in the way of my trade, and many an interesting tale of life on the road did he tell me during the three years we were shopmates.

It has twice fallen to my lot to go on the road. The first occasion was just after I was " out of my time." It was in the month of November. I had just become lord of myself, and was determined to show—by refusing to listen to the advice of disinterested friends, who were older, wiser, and more experienced than myself—that I was a man. Go on the road I would, and go on the road I did; and most sincerely I repented of that same going before many days were over my unhappy head. With a bundle containing a change of clothes under my arm, and in company with a mate who, like myself, was going on the road for the first time, I set out at seven o'clock one clear frosty morning. We had taken a good warm breakfast before starting, and were well under way by daylight. The coldness of the weather necessitating a good pace, we reached the town at which we intended to stay for the night, and which was twenty-eight miles distant, early in the afternoon. After a tea-dinner we rested for an hour, and then went out to a place at which we knew the men of our trade were wont to congregate, in order to get "the tips" as to the probabilities of getting work in that town. We were received by our fellow-craftsmen in all brotherly kindness; but the intelligence they had to give us was not very encouraging, being to the effect that trade was dull, and many men were out of work. There was nothing for us but to continue our journey; and at an early hour next morning we were again on the road. At starting we felt rather sick and footsore; but we got better as we warmed to our work, and after the first five miles got along at a tolerably good rate, though not so quickly as on the day before. Our conversation was also less cheerful and more forced than it had been on the first day, and the night was rapidly closing in when we had done the thirty miles to the town in which we were going to sleep. We were too tired to go out that night, and after a wash and a feed went to bed.

In the morning we were astir in time to meet the workmen coming to their breakfasts; and having ascertained from some of them that trade was tolerably good in the town, we determined to try for work there. Accordingly we called at a number of shops, and at one of them my companion (who belonged to a different branch of the trade from mine) got employed; but I was less fortunate, as every shop was full-handed in my particular line. My companion, though there had been no agreement to that effect, offered to share his wages with me if I liked to stay in the town for a week or two. This liberal offer, however, I declined, and on the following morning I started on my travels alone. Then, for the first time, I began fully to experience the real miseries of being on tramp. I was very footsore; for though I had not been on. the road the day before, I had been walking about the streets of a busy town, and waiting about workshop gates all day—a kind of thing which takes more out of a man on tramp than a day's straightforward walking. Now that I had no one to speak to, each mile seemed as long as two had previously done. I had only got about seven miles on my way when it began to rain heavily, and continued to do so until my clothes were thoroughly saturated; and a cold wind rising as soon as the rain

ceased, my wet clothes were made to cling round me
in a horribly chilling manner. It was dark when,
utterly weary, and beginning to feel uncomfortably
feverish, I reached the town which I had marked
out as my resting-place for the night. Having made
the best of my way to the public-house to which I
had been recommended by one who had " done" the
line of road, I ordered a supper, which, to my surprise, I found I could not eat, and went to bed. To
bed, but not to sleep! the feverish feeling increasing
during the night to an extent that kept me tossing
and tumbling from side to side until daylight began
to dawn, and then I got up, weary and unrefreshed.
Still I was determined to push on, and I once more
set out. The morning was tolerably fine, and the
fresh air revived me considerably; my feet too felt
less painful than they had done on the previous day;
and becoming a little more cheerful on making these
discoveries, I resolved that I would that day " do" the
larger half of the sixty-five miles that still lay between
me and London, in which city I had made up my
mind to wait for work, if I met with none before
reaching it. My spirits rose as I made this resolution, and in imagination I had already reached " the

great city," had been " shopped" at top wages, and
was just in the act of relating some of *my* tramping
adventures to a group of admiring shopmates, when
I was disagreeably startled by the commencement
of a heavy pour of rain, which lasted for several
hours, and by which my clothes were wetted through
and through before I could reach any adequate
shelter. With the chilling of my body came a corresponding chill of spirits and a return of feverish
symptoms, under the influence of which I soon fell
into a very despondent frame of mind; and at
length, about noon, at which time the rain was
still coming down in torrents, I recklessly sat me
down on a large stone by the roadside, with a
vague intention of writing my name and address
on a piece of paper, fastening it to my jacket,
and there and then giving up the ghost. While
searching my pockets for a piece of pencil with
which to carry out the first part of this plan, I
fell to reflecting upon my position; and by some
curious process of reasoning, the method of which
(if it ever had any) I do not now recollect, I fully
persuaded myself that society in general, and not
my own wrong-headedness, was responsible for the

sad case in which I found myself. Strange as it may seem, this idea afforded me consolation, as did also the repetition to myself of some lines that had been composed, under circumstances similar to those in which I then was, by a former shopmate of mine, and which ran thus:

> " Out in the rain, the pitiless rain,
> Suffering from hunger, cold, and pain,
> The weary tramp pursues his way;
> He has travelled many miles to-day,
> And many he must travel yet,
> Though his heart is heavy and garments wet."

By the time I had repeated this doggerel two or three times, and fished out the piece of pencil from the contents of my pockets, a considerable modification had taken place in my views respecting life and death. If I were to die, it occurred to me that I might as well die in harness; while if I were not to die—and I began to suspect that I was by no means so near death as I had a few minutes before supposed—I was only losing time by sitting on a damp stone grumbling. So, taking heart of grace, I rose to my feet again, and walked on till about six o'clock in the evening, when I reached a town in which there was a club-house belonging to my trade. Finding that I could have a bed in that house, I took up my quarters there for the night. After drinking a cup of tea, I leaned my aching head against the back of the screen, and fell into a restless snatchy kind of sleep, from which I was aroused by feeling a cool soft hand laid on my forehead. On looking up, I found that the hand was that of the buxom widow who was the landlady of the house. She was fat, fair, and forty, and had a countenance so comely and so beaming with good-nature, that it was a positive pleasure to look upon it. As I gazed into her kind matronly face, and met her pitying glance, I felt fairly broken down. My troubles had before only tended to make me sullen, and to cause me to bring unfounded charges against society, but the land-lady's touch of nature melted me in an instant, and, but that there were two or three customers looking on, I believe I should have laid my head on her expansive bosom, and had what the ladies call " a good cry."

" Poor boy," she said, when she saw that I was awake, " you're very bad ; but don't be cast down, we'll soon put you to rights again ; come with me, and I'll give you something that will do you good."

I followed her into her own cosy little parlour, where a warm bath for my feet, and a basin of strongly-dashed gruel, were speedily got ready, the servant in the mean time being instructed to take the sheets from the bed in which I was to sleep, and put additional blankets on it. I got to bed with all convenient haste, and had not been long between the blankets, when the landlady's remedies began to have the desired effect. A profuse perspiration, which in all probability saved me from a violent fever, broke out all over me, and lasted for several hours. About midnight I fell into a sound sleep, from which I only awoke at eleven o'clock next day, and then I felt quite restored.

I stayed in the inn all that day, and when going to bed at night intimated to the landlady that I would settle with her then, for I wished to be on the road at an early hour the following morning, as it was my intention to walk to London without further stoppages.

" You had better go by train," she said, when I had told her my intentions, " and not run the risk of knocking yourself up again."

In order that I might not seem to be disregarding

her advice from obstinacy, I hinted that after paying her I feared I should not be able to afford going by train. Upon hearing this, she not only insisted upon my letting her bill stand over until I should get into collar, but even offered to lend me money to pay my fare to London.

"I couldn't afford to lose the money," she said, "and I wouldn't lend it to everyone; but you seem to be a decent, well-spoken lad, and you're fresh from home, and I've lads of my own who'll soon have to go out in the world, and for their sake I wouldn't see any tidy young fellow in difficulties for the sake of a few shillings, if I could help him. Besides," she concluded, with a smile, "I don't think that you would wrong anyone who trusted you."

I fervently assured her, though not exactly in the language of the poet, that even if I *had* a heart for falsehood framed, I ne'er could injure her. I started for London by the first train on the following morning, and two days afterwards got work there. In a few weeks I settled the bill of the warm-hearted landlady, accompanying the money with a present of a "dress-piece," as a token that I had not forgotten the motherly kindness I had received at her hands.

This present she accepted in the spirit in which it was given, though I subsequently ascertained that, owing to my taste in colours being of a decidedly florid order, she was unable to make any use of it, since, as she observed when afterwards speaking to me on the subject, it was a little too flaming for a woman of her years and figure.

My second tramp, though it lasted for five weeks, was much pleasanter than my first, chiefly owing to the circumstances that it took place during the summer, and that I had for a travelling-companion a tramp so experienced that tramping might with him be almost said to be a profession. He was a perfect master of road-craft, and having before been over many of the roads along which we passed, was often acquainted with short cuts that saved several miles in the course of a day's march. He had a practical, if not a scientific, knowledge of physiognomy, never mistaking his man in asking for a " lift." To him, the outsides of houses presented indications of their inhabitants, and he would unhesitatingly " spot" the farm-houses at which by asking for a drink of water you would be sure to get a drink of beer or milk. He carried a small kit of tools with him, and was noted for his skill in repairing beer-engines and other machinery pertaining to the public-house business. In company with such a guide, philosopher, and friend as this, life on the road was comparatively pleasant, and when, after tramping through a great part of Yorkshire and Lancashire, we at last got into collar again in one of the large towns of the latter county, it was almost with a feeling of regret that I once more " buckled to" at the little-varying routine of workshop life.

When a working man on tramp arrives in any town in which men with whom he has formerly " worked mates" are employed, his old shopmates vie with each other who shall be kindest to him. When, by their invitation, he goes to meet them coming from their work, there is a friendly rivalry as to which of them shall take him home to share their meal; and when at night they take him out with them, they display the utmost delicacy in seeing that he is allowed to bear no part of any expenses that may be incurred. If any of them have influence in the establishment in which they are employed, they exert it to the utmost in trying to get work for their old mate; and if he do not obtain employment in the town, and is very hard up, they will make a subscription among themselves, and sometimes among their fellow-workmen, to help him on the road. In such towns as Birmingham, Manchester, and Liverpool, and more especially in the London district, a workman on tramp will, if he is tolerably well known in the trade, and has, when in collar, shown a disposition to assist those who were out, often be kept among his former shopmates, or by those whom in his day he has assisted, until such time as he gets work in the district; and trade must be very dull indeed if in the large towns a man who has friends in the trade on the look-out for work for him does not get into employment in the course of a few weeks. When a man who has been a considerable length of time on the road gets into work again, the kindness and consideration of his fellow-workmen still attend him and do him good service. They will lend him their best tools, and "pitch into" their own work in order to be able to lend him a hand with his, until he has recovered from the effects of his tramp, and got into the ways of the shop; while anyone who attempted to "horse" a man fresh from the road would be scouted by his fellow-craftsmen.* But for such friendly consideration as this, those who have got employment after being on tramp would often be unable to retain it, as life on the road knocks up all men more or less, and for days, and sometimes weeks, renders them incapable of working on equal terms with men who have been living regularly.

Through the influence of former mates who may have been " well in" with the foremen or managers of the shops in which they are employed, or by happening to " drop across" some shop just at the time it is in want of hands, the tramp perhaps gets into work again ; but if after a long tramp he fails to find employment, there is nothing for him to do but to make his way back to his own district, and go into " the big shop"—a shop of which I propose to give some description in the following paper.

* To horse a man, is for one of two men who are engaged on precisely similar pieces of work to make extraordinary exertions in order to work down the other man. This is sometimes done simply to see what kind of a workman a new man may be, but often with the much less creditable motive of injuring a fellow-workman in the estimation of an employer ; with the exception, perhaps, of a skulking fellow who tries to avoid doing his fair share of a joint job, there is no man more despised of working men than the one who tries to horse another for a selfish or spiteful purpose.

IN THE BIG SHOP.

To place one workshop above all others in point of size by calling it *the* "big shop," is a proceeding which, at the first glance, may appear a very defiant challenging of comparison. In this England of ours, whose giant manufactories in every branch of mechanical industry are a chief source of her material wealth, and are justly regarded with feelings of national pride, and by the members of the various trades to which they pertain with personal pride also, a comparison of this kind would to many people appear emphatically odious. It is one, too, you would likely be told that cannot be sustained. Were you to cite some of the great Government establishments, such as the arsenal at Woolwich, or any of the large dockyards, you would be reminded of the great iron, mining, and pottery works of Staffordshire, or the famous breweries of Burton, or the monster factories of Manchester and Birmingham, and building firms of the metropolis, or be asked if the gigantic engineering establishments of the London and North-Western Railway at Crewe and Wolverton did not on an average employ a greater number of hands than any one Government work. Thus, when there are so many big shops, and when, owing to the rapid fluctuations in trade, the shop that is big to-day may be, in respect to the number of men employed in it, small to-morrow, to speak of the "big shop" will to the uninitiated appear a throwing-down of the gauntlet to the admirers and supporters of all workshops above the average size.

But working men will know that nothing of that kind is intended. Compared with the "big shop," as they understand it, all other shops are insignificant; for their big shop has the sky for a roof, and the extent of a great city, or of a district embracing a number of large towns, for its boundaries. It is when a man is out of work at a time when, from there being an extraordinary slap of dull trade, or the particular trade with which he is connected being in a state of decay—such a time as the cotton famine or the period of the fearful distress that more than two years ago came upon the working population of the East of London in consequence of the collapse of the ship-building trade of the Thames, and which still exists among them, unmitigated in extent and constantly increasing in severity—it is when he is out of employment at such sorrowful times as these, when there is nothing for him to do but to wait and suffer until things "right themselves," that a working man is with grim humour said to be in the "big shop."

"Let those abandon hope who enter here," might with much appropriateness and little exaggeration be taken as the motto of the "big shop," for it is indeed a hopeless one—a shop in which the work is as wearying and heartbreaking as it is profitless; for though men know that from the disastrous state of trade it is practically useless to look for work, they desperately continue to hope and try, and day after day walk long distances, and wait patiently for hours outside workshop gates, in vain search for the work they cannot find. A terrible time is it when the "big shop" is "full-handed;" a time to make a brave man eat his heart out, and cause the most cheerful to despond; a time when men not only suffer the woes of want themselves, but are mad-

dened by the sense of their powerlessness to save
their wives and children from those woes; a time
when household gods are shivered, and the comfortable little homes, that it has taken years of industry
to get together, scattered, never perhaps to be re-
formed—furniture and clothing being parted with
to obtain food, and houses abandoned for cheap
rooms; a time when the pawnbrokers' shelves are
crowded with goods pledged at a truly sacrificial
price, and never destined to be redeemed; when the
small shopkeeper is in self-defence compelled to
withhold credit, and the weekly visits of the landlord are looked forward to with fear and trembling;
a time, in short, of poverty, hunger, and general
misery.

One of the worst phases of such times as these is
that a large proportion of the sufferers are people
who have never previously known what it was to be
in absolute distress. There are many of the casually
employed classes, and of the poorer kinds of regular
labourers, and others who are not poor, who habitually prey upon charity, ordinary or special. To
these pauper-souled cormorants the bread of charity
has no bitterness, and they seek it with a shameless,

lying perseverance. They are aware of the existence, and understand the intentions, constitution, and rules, of every local charity, temporary or permanent. They experience no reluctance or sense of shame in appearing before boards or committees, and tell their tales of woe with a glibness and detailed suitability to the resources of the particular charity invoked that *should* excite suspicion ; and knowing "the ropes," they resort to scenic effects if the agents of charity are sent to visit them in their places of abode. Blankets or children's shoes are sent out of the house, the grate is left fireless or the cupboard empty, according to the description of charity over which the visitor has control, and in cases where it is considered safe the number of the family is overstated, and the husband said to be out of work even when he is in. It is these self-degraded dwellers on the threshold of professional mendicancy who in times of special distress among the working classes chiefly profit by the funds which at such times a British public never fails to subscribe. They are the somebodies who get the lion's share of whatever good is blown by these ill winds. Such times to them are as harvest times, during which they wax prosperous and live on the fat of the land. In such times *they* are quite at home, but the really decent mechanic, who in ordinary times has never dreamt of asking for or accepting charity, is " all abroad." The mere idea of charity is hateful to him, and he cannot " put the cheek on" to ask for it ; and as even in their greatest distress he and his family continue to the best of their power to maintain their tidy habits and make the most of whatever is left to them, they fare badly at the hands of charitable visitors, who, as a rule, seem to be of opinion that the greater the dirt and squalor a household displays, the more worthy are its members of charitable relief. The repugnance of the more respectable portion of the working classes to apply for charity, and their anxiety to avoid any unnecessary exposure of their poverty, is not unfrequently attributed to " low pride."

" I've no patience with such ways !" indignantly exclaims some comfortably-situated person, who happens to be aware of the poverty existing in the house of some unemployed artisan, who still strives to appear respectable and independent before the world. " I've no patience with it," they say ; " why, if I was like him, I'd break stones, or sweep a crossing, or do anything, so that it was honest."

Now, this is very fine and very " healthy" talk, but like many other high-sounding generalities, it is *only talk*. Those who are the most ready to indulge in such talk would probably be the first to shrink from its performance were they brought face to face with the reality; and they are generally ignorant of the fact that a man cannot at his own will take to even such callings as stone-breaking or crossing-sweeping. There are vested interests practically equivalent to the rights of proprietorship connected with crossings, and all classes of ordinary labourers object to a mechanic coming among them on the ground that, as he has a trade in his fingers, he should not take the bread out of the mouths of those who have not.

It is chiefly women who indulge in this talk about crossing-sweeping and so forth; but, fortunately for the workmen, their own wives are, as as a rule, too generous and womanly to give way to such senseless reproaches. On the contrary, they are at such times, in the fullest and truest sense, helpmates to their husbands, not only not murmuring

themselves, but cheering and consoling their partners and bearing the brunt of the dreary battle with
poverty. Even the children, in these dark, big-shop
periods, bravely bear, and even strive to alleviate the
sufferings of the family.

At the time when the distress in the East-end of
London was at its worst, I heard one of the destitute
artisans trying to persuade one of his children—a
boy ten years of age—to stay at home and lie down,
instead of going to his work in a chemical factory.
The factory was two miles from his home, the boy
was sickly and feverish, scantily clad, and crippled
from wearing bad shoes, and two small pieces of
dry bread were all that his parents could give him
as food for the day; and altogether he was certainly
much fitter to be in bed than to go to work. But
with a smile on his hunger-pinched countenance he
cheerily answered, " O, I'll go, father; for I know
mother'll be glad of the three shillings on Saturday,
and I'll get butter to my bread again when you get
into work." And so with his bit of bread in his
pocket he trudged off.

And it is in this spirit of resignation and mutual
love and willingness to pull together, men, women,

and children bear their fate in these most miserable times. But however patient and enduring they and their families may be, the resources of a working man soon become utterly exhausted in the " big shop ;" and it is only by the aid of charity, or work specially devised with the view to assisting them, that after the first few months the majority of them can continue to exist.

To be efficient, however, relief to those in the " big shop," no matter of what kind, should be upon a comprehensive scale, controlled by a central organisation, and administered by competent disinterested and unsectarian agents, and should be, in a word, what the Cotton Famine Relief Fund was, but what funds subscribed for similar purposes rarely are.

THE END.